David Friedrich Strauss and His Critics

# American University Studies

Series VII
Theology and Religion
Vol. 16

PETER LANG
New York · Berne · Frankfurt am Main

Edwina G. Lawler

# David Friedrich Strauss and His Critics

## The Life of Jesus Debate in Early Nineteenth-Century German Journals

PETER LANG
New York · Berne · Frankfurt am Main

**Library of Congress Cataloging-in-Publication Data**

Lawler, Edwina
    David Friedrich Strauss and His Critics.

    (American University Studies. Series VII,
Theology and Religion ; vol. 16)
    Bibliography: p.
    Includes index.
        1. Strauss, David Friedrich, 1808-1874. Leben Jesu. 2. Jesus Christ-
Biography. 3. Christian biography.-Palestine. 4. Jesus Christ-Historicity.
5. Theology-Study and teaching-Germany-Periodicals-History-19th century.
I. Title. II. Series: American University Studies. Series VII,
Theology and Religion ; v. 16.
    BT301.S73L38   1986      232.9'01      86-7245
    ISBN 0-8204-0292-7
    ISSN 0740-0446

CIP-Kurztitelaufnahme der Deutschen Bibliothek

**Lawler, Edwina:**
David Friedrich Strauss and His Critics : The Life of Jesus Debate
in Early 19. Century German Journals / Edwina Lawler. - New York ;
Berne ; Frankfurt am Main : Lang, 1986.
    (American University Studies : Ser. 7, Theology and Religion ; Vol. 16)
    ISBN 0-8204-0290-7

NE: American University Studies / 07

© Peter Lang Publishing, Inc., New York 1986

All rights reserved.
Reprint or reproduction, even partially, in all forms such as
microfilm, xerography, microfiche, microcard, offset strictly prohibited.

Printed by Weihert-Druck GmbH, Darmstadt (West-Germany)

Table of Contents

Introduction .................................................... 1

Chapter One
  David Friedrich Strauss - A Biographical
  Sketch ........................................................ 7

Chapter Two
  Sources of Strauss's Concept of Myth ......................... 21

  1. The "Mythic School"
     a. Christian Gottlob Heyne ............................ 23
     b. Eichhorn and Gabler ................................ 24
     c. Georg Lorenz Bauer ................................. 30
     d. Wilhelm de Wette ................................... 31

  2. Ferdinand Christian Baur ............................. 33

  3. The "Mythic Principle" ............................... 34

  4. Das Leben Jesu
     a. Plans for Das Leben Jesu .......................... 39
     b. Strauss's Concept of Myth ......................... 42

Chapter Three
  Critical Response to Das Leben Jesu

  1. Das Leben Jesu seen as Destructive
     Criticism ............................................ 47

  2. Dogmatic Assumptions Precluding
     Acceptance of the Mythic View ........................ 50
     a. Johann Christian Friedrich Steudel ................ 53
     b. Carl Friedrich Stäudlin ........................... 54
     c. Ernst Friedrich Gelpke ............................ 56
     d. Johann Tobias Beck ................................ 58
     e. Carl Ullmann ...................................... 59
     f. Summary ........................................... 63

  3. Speculative and Empirical Presuppositions
     Found Operative in Strauss ........................... 65
     a. Concept of Religion ............................... 69
     b. Representation and Concept ........................ 71
     c. Problem of the Archetype .......................... 78
     d. Problem of Development ............................ 89
     e. Miracles .......................................... 94

  4. Concept of Myth and the Myth-Forming Process.......... 99

Chapter Four
  Conclusion ..................................................117

Explanation of Abbreviations .................................. 123
Notes ...,..................................... 125
Bibliography .................................. 139
Index ......................................... 147
Appendix ...................................... 149

Introduction

Just as the work of Immanuel Kant can be viewed as the culmination of the German Enlightenment, so, too, can Friedrich Nietzsche's proclamation of the death of God be viewed with regard to a speculative process of thought made possible by the limits imposed on reason by Kant's critique of this human faculty. Among the nineteenth century thinkers who prepared the ground for Nietzsche's oft-quoted conclusion was David Friedrich Strauss who in 1835 published his <u>Life of Jesus Critically Examined</u>. The myth-forming process described here by Strauss and his application of it to the biblical narratives led Strauss to conclusions which were the highpoint and culmination of the tendency begun in the eighteenth century to allow for mythic interpretations of the Bible.

This study approaches Strauss's <u>Leben Jesu</u> through the criticism levelled against it in theological and philosophical German journals in the first half of the nineteenth century. In order to put Strauss's work in an historical context a discussion of the leading eighteenth century positions on myth and the Bible precedes it.

As could be expected, the critical response to Strauss's work was essentially negative. Strauss was caught in a crossfire between mediating theologians and the supernaturalist theologians of his time. The mediating theologians, whether of the neo-Schleiermacherian or of the right-wing Hegelian variety, attempted to restate the super-naturalism of church doctrine in terms of modern philosophy. They attributed supernatural characteristics to the historical Christ because their view of idealism allowed them to make a total identification of the archetypal and the historical.

For these mediating theologians Strauss's consistent mythical interpretation of the Gospels represented the dissolution of any such synthesis between the archetypal and the historical by either Schleiermacher or Hegel. On the other hand, the mediating theologians opposed the reactionary tendencies of conservative protestant theology, such as that represented by the Lutheran <u>Evangelische Kirchenzeitung</u> and the <u>Zeitschrift für Protestantismus und Kirche</u>.

The supernaturalist theologians rejected the idea of a complete identification of the archetypal and the historical, holding rather to the belief that the supernatural character of Christianity always remains the same. Any historical alterations or apparent changes come only as a result of the human subjectivity that entertains the supernatural essence of the faith. The orthodox view of supernaturalism would not admit that human subjectivity played such a conditioned role.

Since neither Strauss nor his critics could totally free themselves from dogmatic and/or speculative assumptions, their attempts at historical criticism remain flawed. The hold of idealism, of the idea and its realization is revealed in their respective critical arguments. Strauss's critical examination was conditioned not only by the identification of representation and myth but also by the manner in which for him the idea of the God-man is realized in history. In the case of the critics it is both the manner of the realization of this idea, and the related need for an absolute religion that are determinative. Nevertheless, Strauss proves to be truer to the historical enterprise than were his critics. In his account of the myth-forming process Strauss anticipates current thinking in biblical criticism, e.g., studies on the Midrash character of the Gospels and aspects of redaction criticism.

The critics of Strauss considered here include the following. Ferdinand Christian BAUR (1792-1860), who advocated a consistently historical view of the New Testament, was a primary influence on the Tübingen school of biblical criticism. His concept of history as movement through conflict was influenced by Hegel. Johann Tobias BECK (1809-78), professor of theology in Basel and later Tübingen, was a primary representative of an anti-rationalistic biblicism. After being released from Berlin in 1819 for political reasons, Wilhelm Martin Leberecht DE WETTE (1780-1849) became professor of theology at Basel. He was a mediating theologian who represented an idealistic-aesthetic symbolism based on feeling as the ground of religious ideas and divination. Johann Philipp GABLER (1753-1826), an advocate of a rational Christianity, allowed for the possibility of saga and/or historical myths in the infant narratives as well as revelation. Samuel Robert GEIER was a teacher at the Latin School for Orphans in Halle and contributor to <u>Zeitschrift für die</u>

historische Theologie. Ernst Friedrich GELPKE (1807-71), professor of theology in Bern, was a mediating theologian influenced by Schleiermacher and Neander. August HAHN (1792-1863), a proponent of biblical supranaturalism, advocated the removal of rationalists from the church. Heinrich KERN, one of Strauss's teachers in Blaubeuren and Tübingen, was co-editor of the Tübinger Zeitschrift für Theologie. Julius MUELLER (1801-78), professor of theology at Halle, was a mediating theologian influenced by Schleiermacher. He made the doctrine of sin the center of his dogmatics; in the knowledge of sin the necessity of an objective, divine revelation becomes clear. Edgar QUINET, a Frenchman, was a Catholic poet. In 1851, Daniel SCHENKEL (1813-85) was called to a professorate in theology in Heidelberg. His liberal theological views were influenced by de Wette. In his criticism of Das Charakterbild Jesu (1864) Strauss accused Schenkel of camouflaging a non-belief in the supernatural character of Jesus. Alexander SCHWEIZER (1808-88), professor in Zürich, was one of Schleiermacher's most faithful pupils. He developed a Christology that reflected his idea of the religious as an area in which the effect and the force of genial personalities was especially strong. Carl Friedrich STAEUDLIN (1761-1826), professor of theology in Göttingen, was a believer in revealed religion who attempted to combine rational-critical philosophy in the Kantian sense with Christian teaching. Johann Christian Friedrich STEUDEL (1779-1837), professor of theology in Tübingen, was the last representative of Gottlob Christian Storr's supranaturalism. Carl ULLMANN (1796-1865), professor of theology in Heidelberg and later in Halle, was co-founder of <u>Theologische Studien und Kritiken</u>. He was a mediating theologian who affirmed Schleiermacher's emphasis on subjective religious experience rooted in feeling but considered religious feeling the source of objective knowledge. His dogmatics aimed at bringing a modified supranaturalism into harmony with the contemporary critical spirit. Leonard USTERI (1799-1834), professor and director of the secondary school in Berne, allowed for mythical elements in the New Testament. Friedrich VORLAENDER was a contributor to <u>Zeitschrift für Philosophie und spekulative Theologie</u>. Christian Hermann WEISSE (1801-1866) was a professor of philosophy at Leipzig and, together with I. H. Fichte, the most significant representative of speculative theism.

Unless an English translation of a German work is indicated, all translations of German material is by this author. The original German for the English translations can be found in the notes. A translation of the article entitled "Die verschiedenen Rücksichten aus welchen und für welche der Biograph Jesu arbeiten kann" appears in full in the appendix. It is one of the more significant articles because of its succinct assessment of the theological climate of the age.

Chapter One

In 1835, David Friedrich Strauss published the first volume of Das Leben Jesu. Aspects of Christianity had been called into question before but never had the Gospel stories of Jesus been subjected to such radical and penetrating criticism as in Das Leben Jesu. Strauss's examination of the Gospel narratives compelled the 27 year old author to repudiate the authenticity and therewith the authority of the Gospels, the very foundation on which the doctrines of Christianity stood. His contemporaries responded quickly. In 1836, Heinrich Kern asserted that anyone who participated in the progress of theology had to come to terms with the criticism exercised in this work.[1] Carl Ullmann considered Strauss's undertaking capable of attracting general attention even in a political-industrial age and of providing the occasion for significant articles in the field of theology.[2]

Between 1836 and 1843, four reviews and twenty-three essays dealing with Das Leben Jesu were published in four journals. Three reviews and nine essays appeared in Theologische Studien und Kritiken; one review and five essays, in Zeitschrift für Philosophie und spekulative Theologie; two essays, in Zeitschrift für die historische Theologie; and seven essays, in <u>Tübinger Zeitschrift für Theologie</u>. The critics were understandably disturbed by the results of Strauss's investigation of the biblical narratives and realized that the scientific thoroughness of the work did not permit dismissing it as a piece of heretical fantasy. In response to the work, articles were written to show why a purely historical approach to the Gospels was inappropriate. Other critics sprang to the attack, pointing to the speculative and empirical presuppositions of Strauss's alleged presuppositionless work, and marshalled arguments against them. Strauss's application of his concept of myth was questioned, and while the vitality of myth was emphasized by some writers, others asserted the non-mythic nature of the Gospels. In general, critics considered Strauss's work a piece of destructive criticism: Strauss wanted to resolve the biblical narratives into myths and reduce the historical Jesus to an idea in order to remove one of the greatest obstacles, if not the greatest, for speculative philosophy: the person of Jesus of Nazareth as the incarnate God.

Before considering the criticism of <u>Das Leben Jesu</u>, Strauss himself deserves to be heard not only with respect to his work but also with respect to his person. Objectivity is expected in a scientific undertaking, but because of the nature of the object under investigation, the objectivity of <u>Das Leben Jesu</u> could easily be mistaken for callous insensitivity, and indifference to beliefs long held by the Christian Church.

## A. Strauss on Strauss

### 1. Early Years

Strauss attributed his unhappiness, his prevailing mood of sorrow, and his total inability to enjoy life to the fact that he was conceived at a time when his parents were inconsolably saddened by the death of their eight year old son Fritz.[3] Because of his love for Latin and innate understanding of every kind of literature, Strauss's father, Johann Friedrich, should have pursued a scholarly life; instead, he followed tradition and became a merchant.[4] In 1814, he inherited the business of his stepfather but had little talent for the practicalities of buying and selling. His free-time activities (fruit trees, bees, ancient and modern poetry, mysticism) drew him farther and farther from his business. Thus, it fell to Strauss's mother, Christiane, to keep the business and the family's financial situation from bankruptcy. What enabled Strauss's mother to maintain her tranquility and cheerfulness amidst financial difficulties were constant, dutiful activity and trust in a wise and benevolent providence which, she believed, would right everything provided one met one's responsibilities.

Such a religion of conscientious action and trust in providence was insufficient for Strauss's father. He required something outside of himself: Christ's propitiating death. While Johann Friedrich speculated on Christ, His divine nature, His holy name, His world-redeeming sacrifice, Christiane saw in

Christ a wise teacher sent by God, a virtuous man whose martyrdom was of little help if one did not imitate His teaching and follow His example. Both the mystic, introspective, reflective tendency of his father and the practical, rationalistic perspective of his mother were present in Strauss. The latter was the more dominant, but the former was never totally overcome.

## 2. Blaubeuren and Tübingen

In 1821, at the age of 13, Strauss entered Blaubeuren, one of the four junior seminaries in Württemberg. Among his teachers were Heinrich Kern and Ferdinand Christian Baur, both of whom were to join the Protestant theological faculty at the university in Tübingen after Strauss had matriculated there. In his memorials to Christian Märklin and Justinus Kerner, Strauss recalls his days at Tübingen (1825-29).[5]

At that time the theological program at Tübingen lasted five years. The first two years were devoted to philosophy, including philology and history, and the last three years, to theology. Philosophy as taught at Tübingen did not go much beyond Schelling and occupied a position subservient to the rationalized supernaturalism espoused by the theological faculty. The situation was remedied in 1826 when Kern and Baur were appointed to the theological faculty to replace Bengel who had died. The old Tübingen School that started with Storr died with Steudel. With Baur and his disciples a new Tübingen School appeared. Kant, Jacobi, and Schelling were read. Kant had little appeal for the youth raised in Swabia where romanticism, supernaturalism, and mysticism were at home. The very fact that anyone would want to establish limits to the human faculty of knowing was in itself perplexing to Strauss. The natural philosophy of Schelling proved more palatable. But when he discovered Jacob Böhme, his enthusiasm turned from Schelling to one who actually saw living forces within himself and in nature.[6]

Through his study of Böhme, Strauss acquired a strong supernatural belief which stemmed from the conviction that Böhme penetrated more deeply into the nature of God than did the Bible. Soon the desire for direct knowledge of truth and of the divine led to dissatisfaction with Böhme; what was immediate knowledge for him was mediated to Strauss through the most lifeless of means, the written word. Strauss now wanted personal contact with a contemporary who had the direct intuition of a Jacob Böhme. Justinus Kerner introduced Strauss and his friends to a somnambulist who lived in the nearby town of Weinsberg.[7] During the visit the seeress was transported into a magnetic sleep, and Strauss himself was put into a magnetic rapport with her. He recalled having passed the test well. Strauss visited the seeress often, but never again did he experience the exultation or intensity of that first visit.

In the meantime the direction of his studies had changed: the darkness of Schelling, Böhme, somnambulism, and magnetism was replaced by the light of Schleiermacher. Initial rejection of Schleiermacher was gradually replaced by acceptance, and

Strauss found himself on new intellectual ground; his experiences with somnambulism and magnetism lost all trace of credibility. From Schleiermacher Strauss learned to understand religion in its distinctiveness and to comprehend, to analyze, and to examine theological ideas in their historical character. Zeller explained the attraction and the liberating influence:

> As a philosopher, his [Schleiermacher's] pantheism aroused confidence in the disciple of Schelling; as a theologian, he met the religious devotee and mystic with his Christian knowledge; as an author, he attracted the romanticist by the aesthetic form of his discourses and soliloquies; whilst at the same time, with the acuteness of his logic, he severed the thread, one after the other, which had hitherto bound the mind of his disciple to unproved hypotheses and indistinct ideas.[8]

Gradually Strauss began to feel uneasy with Schleiermacher; his study of Schleiermacher gave him:

> double incentive to press forward where the master rather arbitrarily, so it seemed to us, had set boundaries. The eternal peace which he prided himself on having concluded between philosophy and theology seemed to us to be only a fragile truce. We found it advisable to guard against the event of war.[9]

In Das Leben Jesu Strauss would demonstrate how "fragile" this "eternal peace" was; additional philosophical weapons, however, were still needed, and thus it was that a group of friends, among them Strauss and Märklin, began to meet twice weekly to pursue further their philosophical interests.[10]

They commenced with Kant's Prolegomenen and then turned to Hegel's Phänomenologie. At that time Hegel was virtually unknown in Tübingen. Schneckenburger, a tutor, was the first to lecture on Hegel, and Zimmerman was the first among the friends to proclaim the greatness of this philosopher over the favorites of the others: Schleiermacher, Twesten, Schelling, Franz Baader. The effect of the Phänomenologie was unparalleled:

> While the understanding was absorbed in the strictest dialectical school, the deepest suspicions were offered to the spirit, the most surprising prospects, to the imagination. All of world history passed by us; art and religion in their different forms emerged in their place. And this entire wealth of figures emerged from One Self-consciousness and returned into it again and again. Therewith, it knew itself as the force of all things.[11]

Since final examinations were approaching, the friends then turned to Marheineke, and they were amazed that Hegel had not found a better theological interpreter.

After passing his examinations with distinction, Strauss was appointed to a small church in Klein-Ingersheim. In a letter to Märklin, Strauss indicated that he was continuing his study of Schleiermacher and Hegel, particularly of the latter's Logik.[12] In December 1830, Strauss again wrote to Märklin in response to questions from the latter. In this letter Strauss revealed his understanding of the dilemma in which the speculative theologian found himself vis-à-vis orthodoxy. Hegel differentiated between BEGRIFF or concept and VORSTELLUNG or representation and maintained that religion and philosophy shared the same content, but the form for each was different. Märklin, Strauss explained, was perplexed because he accepted the universal and did not know how he in good conscience could present the particular, the representation, as the essential element to his parishioners. Strauss replied that the universal also comprehended its particular moments which corresponded to the individual moments of the representation so that the latter were not unessential.

Märklin, Strauss continued, found himself in a conflict that was historically necessary. Strauss offered four ways out of the dilemma: 1) to force oneself back to faith which was impossible; 2) to rationalize faith which would be shameful; 3) to leave the ministry which would be radical; 4) to remain aware of the unity in this conflict, of the identity of concept and representation. Just as religion had several forms, so, too, did Christianity have several stages; the present stage hovered between representation and concept. A process of development was necessary, and the individual pastor could not arbitrarily rush this process but for the time being had to preach according to the forms of representation. At the same time, he should let the concept shimmer through the representation as much as possible, and his decision as to what was to be done and how this was to be achieved was dependent on how it would be received by the congregation. Strauss considered any other solution to the problem risky.[13]

In May of 1831, Strauss informed Märklin of his plans to go to Berlin to learn philosophy from the master himself.[14] He heard two lectures by Hegel and then learned from Schleiermacher of the former's death. His first inclination was to return home, but he finally decided to remain in Berlin. It was while he was in Berlin that Strauss revealed his plans to present a series of lectures on the life of Jesus. The lectures never materialized, but the plan in a revised form became Das Leben Jesu.

### 3. The "Artistic Scientist"

As a result of the unfavorable reception of Das Leben Jesu, Strauss was relieved of his teaching responsibilities at the Tübingen seminary and assigned to a high school in Ludwigsburg where he remained for barely a year. In September, 1836, he moved to Stuttgart to work as a private scholar and writer, the profession that was to be his for the rest of his life. After three unsuccessful attempts initiated by his friends to have him appointed to the university in Zürich, Strauss never again tried to become part of the academic world.[15] Nor would he be offered, as he well knew, a position in the church. In late summer 1842, Strauss married Agnese Schebest, a renowned and rightly acclaimed singer. Their marriage ended in a divorce four years later.

Strauss was given custody of his two children, Fritz and Georgine. In 1848, Strauss was actively involved in politics as a member of the Württemberg Diet, and in 1870, his published correspondence with Renan in which he eloquently and emphatically expressed his national sentiments caused him to attain once again fleeting acclamation in the political scene. Strauss spent his life wandering from Stuttgart to Munich, to Weimar and Heidelberg, to Berlin, to Darmstadt, and finally back to Ludwigsburg, sometimes in search of a topic on which he could work, sometimes intimately involved with research and writing, always interested in music and art, frequently disappointed about the unfavorable reaction to his publications, occasionally pleased that a work was well received. He was a man without a home physically, emotionally, and intellectually.

Strauss referred to himself as an artistic scientist.[16] He confessed that the scientific work he did was done from passion, and that without passion, he could do nothing. This he regarded as the artistic element in his nature. But at the same time he admitted that he was even less a poet than a scholar because he totally lacked the productivity of fantasy and the creative force.[17] In him fantasy was a vacuum, at best the gift of metaphor, of image, but only as something accidental or decorative. And yet, he wrote, it was the bit of a poet in him that formed the foundation on which his intellectual life was built.[18]

For Strauss the artist outranked the scientist. In <u>Dem Alten und dem Neuen Glauben</u> Strauss presented artists as replacements for lost religious ideals, artists in whose works he had found a harmonious worldview in which man, while developing his higher faculties, still remained one with nature. He ranked Goethe higher than Hegel, Shakespeare higher than Spinoza, Sophocles higher than Aristotle because he was convinced that the cooperation of unconscious instinctive forces with and in the pure service of conscious rational forces was of more value than the activity of the latter in and of itself. For him Schiller's statement that the philosopher was always only half a man and only the poet was a whole man was irrefutable.[19]

The feeling and sensitivity associated with the artistic was also evident in Strauss's intellectual development and scholarly publications. Initially only a system that appealed primarily to feeling and to representational thought attracted him; thus Jacobi, Schelling, Böhme, Kerner. What initially attracted Strauss to Schleiermacher was the artistic style of the latter; with Hegel, his passion for philosophical and theological study properly began.[20] Personal considerations were decisive in the selection of potential biographical material: his subjects had to be warm personalities who were full of life and revealed human nature as such, i.e., unmutilated and unrefined. The intellectual attraction for the subjects of his biographies also included a subjective element; the hero of his biography had to show intellectual interests and deeds that were related to those of

Strauss: "he had to be turned towards light, towards freedom; he had to be an enemy of despots and parsons."[21] Strauss referred to Das Leben Jesu as an "inspired book"[22] and wrote Den Alten und den Neuen Glauben out of the sense of guilt he felt for the spiritual need and emptiness he had occasioned.[23] Strauss recognized that his particular talent lay in the compilation of materials which, in turn, provided the content for creative formation.[24] This talent is evident in Das Leben Jesu and in his biographies of Schubart, Hutten, and Frischlin.

Strauss worked in both philosophy and theology. However much he tried to free himself from theology, however often he maintained to have lost interest in theology and in theological questions, his main discipline was theology. To Vischer he wrote: "I have no talent for philosophy as such,"[25] a correct ascertainment since, as is evident in Dem Alten und dem Neuen Glauben, he lacked the ability to develop a consistent system; in the field of literature he was, as he maintained in the same letter and often repeated, a dilettante; he was not, as he himself acknowledged, an historian, for he could not suspend a dogmatic interest.[26] In 1843, Strauss admitted to his brother Wilhelm that only in theology could he accomplish something fundamental.[27]

Strauss understood himself well. Schleiermacher, Harris wrote, may have been the greatest theologian of the nineteenth century; Baur, the most influential; but Strauss was "the most important theological personality during the middle half of the century," as well as "the most interesting."[28] Müller speaks for many when he writes that Strauss did not have "that deeper impartial understanding for the unique mode of the theological and the religious."[29] In a technical sense and from an orthodox perspective this may, in fact, be a valid assessment. But it is equally true that Strauss grappled throughout his life with the problem of the absolute and attempted to reconcile religion with modern consciousness, to demonstrate scientifically that one could still believe if and once one was convinced of the truth of that in which one believed. That a gulf came to exist between Strauss and theology was due to Strauss himself. Strauss wrote:

> Again and again I return from the accusation of
> fate to the self-accusation that I should have
> been more persistent and less sensitive,
> that I should have continued to spin from
> the thread which I had once grasped firmly.[30]

CHAPTER TWO

Sources of Strauss's Concept of Myth

With the general advances made in the study of nature and in historical studies, it was perhaps unavoidable that biblical statements that seemed to contradict this knowledge would be pronounced erroneous and set aside as uninspired. The area of religious truth was defined within the limits of reason, and in the course of criticism this area dwindled considerably. The reality of miracles was questioned by the rationalists who sought natural explanations for them. Then the representations of the divine and of divine action became the object of criticism. The criterion as to what was acceptable was taken from the Bible itself: the New Testament concepts were considered purer than Old Testament concepts, and in the New Testament the teachings of Jesus were contrasted with those of the Apostles.[31] As reason became more and more aware of itself and confident in the applicability of its own criteria and principles in the area of religion, criticism became all-encompassing. From the basis of natural religion, attempts were made to ascertain what was true and false and what could be regarded as revelation.

At first error was attributed to the subjectivity of the biblical authors. Anything deemed erroneous was considered under one of three categories: deception and lie, conscious accommodation to the listener's level of intelligence, or the level of knowledge at that time. The first consideration was seen as improbable and contradictory to the moral spirit advanced in the Bible. If conscious accommodation could not be read directly from the text, it could not be used as an explanation. Effectively only the third consideration, that of the level of knowledge, remained.[32] This led to the comparison of biblical and non-biblical representations of the miraculous among primitive peoples; the same structure of all such representations and the universality of this kind of representation were observed.

In the study of antiquity the term myth was used for heroic stories and for traditional narratives about the direct intervention and the miraculous works of divinity in the world. The application of the concept of myth to the Bible followed from the insight into the common structure of the manner of depiction and narration in the stories of classical antiquity and those of the Bible. With this insight a possibility of interpretation was offered that removed exegesis from the constraining position of having to attribute errors to deceptive intentionality and accommodation.

1. The "Mythic School"[33]

   a. Christian Gottlob Heyne

The eighteenth century classical philologist Christian Gottlob Heyne (1729-1812) became convinced that myth was the universal mode of thinking and expression in the ancient world. On the basis of this conviction, he developed a comprehensive theory of myth.

According to Heyne the mythic mode of thought was the universal mode of thinking and expression in humanity's infancy. It reflected the deficiencies common to all primitive thought: 1) lack of knowledge which prevented knowing true casuality; 2) an inability to think in abstract, universal terms; and 3) the inability to objectify immediate sense impressions which implied an intensified affectibility through the senses.[34] As the necessary early stage in the development of the human process of thinking, the myth precluded any specifically creative or poetic intentionality. While the myth was a poetic form, its poetic character was unintentional and simply reflected the primitive level of thought.

With this view of myth as unintentional poetry, biblical passages which were thought to contain any mythic elements of depiction or speech could no longer be interpreted as allegory. An allegorical interpretation was appropriate only where an allegorical intention on the part of the poet could be proven, and

Heyne's critical interpretation specifically aimed at separating the preliterary, unintentional mythic material from any conscious, poetic transformation.[35]

For Heyne there were two kinds of myth: 1) historical myth at the basis of which was an actual event and 2) philosophical myth which contained ethical speculation or speculation relative to the explanation of natural phenomena.[36] His hermeneutic requirement of investigating myths with respect to their content in order to separate fact from philosophy was to become the modus operandi: each decision as to what was historical and factual and what was the mythic guise concealing opinions or philosophical thought on the part of the biblical authors affected any judgment about the nature of revelation in the biblical passages in question.

Because of his insight into the historically necessary and universal character of mythic thinking and expression which preceded every other kind of poetry, Heyne succeeded in overcoming the rationalistic view of myth according to which everything that was mythic could be grasped only as poetic, i.e., as a product of artistic intentionality in the use of symbol and allegory.

b. Eichhorn and Gabler

Johann Gottfried Eichhorn (1752-1827) introduced Heyne's mythic interpretation into biblical scholarship. His influence on what Hartlich and Sachs termed the "mythic school" was extended by the appearance of his Urgeschichte which he first published anonymously and which was later republished by Johann Philipp Gabler (1753-1826) between 1790 and 1793. Because of their more comprehensive historical conception and more consistent application of it, Eichhorn and Gabler overcame any remaining rationalistic element in biblical exegesis which sought to explain the temporal conditionality of biblical representations as intentional accommodation to local and temporal factors. Accommodation as a general theory was refuted.[37]

Gabler established a necessary principle for the application of mythic interpretation in biblical exegesis in his Altdorfer inaugural address of 1787. Here he stated that exegesis was not dependent on dogmatics, but rather dogmatics was dependent on exegesis.[38] Strauss would also insist on freedom from dogmatic restriction. In his interpretation of the Old Testament Gabler, like Eichhorn, followed the principles set down by Heyne. Their criteria for the classification of myth into the historical, the poetic, and the philosophical were also based on Heyne. Historical myth was defined as the narration of an actual event in the primitive world in the sensual, figurative, visual, and dramatic language and style characteristic of that age; what was narrated was presented as fact. True historical representation was not to be expected; what was to be expected was a true historical basis and a representation of the event that corresponded to the poverty in concept and word, the unfamiliarity with natural causality, and the completely sensual mode of thinking characteristic of primitive man. Since poetic and philosophical myths could also appear as history, the intention of the author to present true history was the central issue in investigating the nature of historical myths. The connection, the guise, and the inner probability of the narrated event were carefully studied.[39] According to Gabler, Eichhorn was the first one to subject biblical myths to such careful scrutiny; before him, all myths were considered true history, and the Bible was thereby delivered to the ridicule of its enemies.[40]

Poetic myth was defined either as an old myth that was poetically embellished or as the composite of several old myths which the poet had combined and adorned so that it appeared as a new composition. There were also poetic myths that were purely poetic products. In the poetic myth, poetic imagination was found either in the fictional element, in the adornment or combination, or in the representation of mythic ideas.[41]

Two kinds of philosophical myths were designated; each had two subdivisions. 1) A philosophical myth could originate from speculation about the causes of finite things or from that about moral objects. The speculative thoughts were then clothed in history. For this type of myth, either the content was presented as conceived, that is, as an idea, or history became the shell for the ideas. 2) A philosophical myth could also arise in such a way that history was basic to it; the poet either expanded history for his own intention or interwove it into his own ideas or opinions.[42] This second type of philosophical myth closely resembled history; it differed from the historical myth in that in the latter, the main emphasis was on the narration of an event, whereas in the former, the author proceeded from his thoughts, used an old saga as his foundation, and developed it for his own dogmatic intention. Both external and internal features had to be considered in order to classify a myth properly. Only after the dominant idea was found, could one determine whether the myth was historical or philosophical.

His insistence on consistency in applying the concept of myth to the works of all primitive peoples led Eichhorn to conclude that the Hebrews did not stand in a privileged position with respect to God. By rejecting the literal truth of the Bible, Eichhorn lent support to the naturalists. But with respect to the theory of deceptive intentionality, Eichhorn and Gabler gave the defenders of the Bible a weapon against the naturalists by asserting that the mythic form of thinking and expression was a necessary, early form of thought in the development of reason. The naturalists claimed that the faculty of reason was the same in all ages and that it was only from error or dishonesty that one could maintain what was contrary to the rules of reason and nature. They, therefore, concluded that the biblical authors were guilty either of absurdity, incongruity, or deception. With the mythic concept this theory could be disputed: because the mythic interpreters insisted on the unintentional, unconscious necessity of the figurative, mythic mode of representation and style, any argument based on the subjectivity of the writer was ineffective. The question of polytheism versus monotheism was irrelevant to the mythic interpretation. Mythic interpreters classified a narrative as myth if in it an event was referred to the direct intervention of divinity without any regard for natural, intermediary causes. It was of no consequence whether this divinity was presented as one god or many. Hess attempted to reject the whole idea of myth on this basis, and of him Strauss remarked: "Hess was by no means the last orthodox theologian who pretended to combat the mythical view with such weapons."[43]

Heyne considered myth to be connected with the preliterary period and limited his application of myth to the Old Testament. Eichhorn and Gabler, however, found mythic forms of representation and expression throughout the entire Bible. Sections in the New Testament that immediately lent themselves to mythic interpretation were: 1) passages that contained an element already recognized as myth; 2) passages that contained certain representational groupings which were automatically to be classified as myth, e.g., direct intervention of divinity; and 3) passages that dealt with the miraculous.

In <u>Journal für auserlesene theologische Literatur</u>, Gabler dealt with two questions relevant to the mythic view: 1) Why were myths only recently found in the Bible? and 2) Even if myths were present in the Old Testament, was it not incorrect, or at least audacious, to assume myths in the New Testament?[44]

In response to the first question, Gabler maintained that the knowledge gained from the more exact study of nature, man, and the world and the more dignified view of God and His properties made it increasingly difficult to consider as true what contradicted the physical and moral nature of man, the natural laws, or the wisdom and holiness of God. What led to the mythic interpretation was, thus, a more exact philosophy of nature and religion and a more fundamental study of the historical documents of ancient peoples and of classical literature. Gabler stressed that the sole intent behind the mythic interpretation was to save the Bible from ridicule and to guarantee to it the respect it deserved. Only if the documents of Christianity were explained as analogous to the literature of other ancient peoples, could this respect be retained.

As for the second question, Gabler considered two frequently raised objections: 1) the designation was inappropriate and 2) the term was startling and unnecessarily sensational.

Myth, Gabler replied, was generally understood to mean one of two things: 1) the treatment of a supersensible object which resembled an historical presentation or 2) miraculous narratives that had their origin in a preliterary period. It was the second meaning that applied to the New Testament narratives that were then being designated myths. Although history was being recorded when Christianity began, no written records existed concerning the early conditions of Jesus' life. About this period only orally transmitted sagas existed. These were subsequently embellished with inferences that supplemented the lack of history. These conjectures and reasonings that corresponded to the Jewish-Christian taste assumed, as was generally true of philosophical myths, the form and character of history. In this way a new kind of myth about primitive Christianity arose: the orally transmitted sagas which were embellished and moved into the realm of the miraculous became historical myths. These myths were distinguished from genuinely historical narratives not by the miraculous which was mutually shared but by the clear traces of Jewish ideas and prejudices, consequently, by factual incorrectness. As to the second objection, Gabler cautioned against using the term with the laity who could too easily be misled to declare the entire Bible a fable because of a few unessential components that were to be called mythic.

c. Georg Lorenz Bauer

In <u>Entwurf einer Hermeneutik des Alten und Neuen Testaments</u> (1799) and <u>Hebraischer Mythologie des Alten und Neuen Testaments, mit Parallelen aus der Mythologie anderer Völker, vornehmlich der Griechen und Römer</u> (1802), Georg Lorenz Bauer (1755-1806) systematically developed the work done by proponents of mythic interpretation into a comprehensive theory and then applied it. His concept of myth and its application to the Bible essentially followed the line already discussed. The decisive criterion for Bauer as to whether that which was narrated was myth or history was the ascertainability of the probability of the narrated event.

Since in Bauer's view it belonged to the essence of primitive thought to attribute human insights and knowledge to divine influence, Bauer considered inspiration itself a myth.[45] Mythic interpretation was no longer restricted to exegesis but had broadened its scope to include dogmatic pronouncements.

            d.  Wilhelm Martin Leberecht de Wette

With de Wette (1780-1849), the concept of myth lost much of its underlying rationalistic tone. De Wette proceeded not from individual narratives but from a mythic whole that was perceived to be basic to the individual mythic stories. For de Wette the Pentateuch, e.g., was historical poetry, specifically the Jewish national epic of theocracy basic to which was the leading idea of the special election of the Jewish people on the part of God. With this theory of a mythic whole permeating particular myths, a devaluation of the particular myths entered criticism to the extent that the communication of this basic idea became the main task of interpretation. The separation of historical facticity and mythic structure in particular narratives lost ground, since in light of such a total mythic perception the critical attempt at separation no longer had a secure point of departure. For de Wette this inseparability from the historical belonged to the essence of myth.[46] Meyer, on the other hand, undertook a defense of the mythic interpretation of particular narratives. This dispute between the mythic school and de Wette was not without significance; it marked:

> the first station in the discussion about the relationship of myth and history, which, with the introduction of the concept of myth into biblical criticism, had to become an inevitable problem. And this occurred precisely on the basis of a shared fundamental view for which the <u>presence</u> of mythic ccmponents in the Bible no longer represented a question.[47]

With the concept of the creative story-producing potency of myth, the division into philosophical myth and historical myth was shaken. Historical myth ceased to be a meaningful classification equal to the philosophical myth, for within a complex of myths that had an historical appearance the particular myth was seen as having a purely mythic basis, i.e., the apparently historical individual myth was understood as the product of a total mythic idea that had an historical-philosophical character, historical only in the sense of conveying the spirit of the people. This marked a significant change. Up to this point, the concept of myth was rationalistic, i.e., myth was seen as a form of reason in its infancy. As mankind developed, so, too, did human reason. Thus, the myth had no independent meaning but was a step in the development of mankind that had to be overcome. With de Wette myth became a unique and independent phenomenon of the human spirit, founded in the inner nature of man: it was the expressive category of religious life. For de Wette myth was the only form, however unsuitable it might be, for conveying the relationship between the eternal and the finite because myth was the free poetic use of supersensible images as they related to the finite. According to de Wette myth was anchored in the anthropological structure of the human faculty of knowing.

De Wette acknowledged basic differences in man's relation to myth: there was a naive, a dogmatic, and a critical use of myth. Myth was used naively in religious poetry that moved unconsciously and poetically in the medium of imagery. The dogmatic use of myth was the false use of mythic images in which the images were taken for the object itself. The critical use of myth was the ideal-aesthetic understanding of mythic imagery based on philosophical insight into its origin and limits.[48]

### 2. Ferdinand Christian Baur

Strauss named all of the above as his predecessors in the application of the concept of myth in biblical exegesis and faulted them either for not conceiving the myth purely enough or for not applying it comprehensively enough. (Only the second accusation applied to de Wette.) In his work Identität und Immanenz, Müller suggests a dependence of Strauss on Baur's Symbolik und Mythologie (1824-25).[49] For Baur (1792-1860), myth was the figurative representation of an idea through an action; it did not reflect real, external history but reflected in an image of an external action the unhistorical, immanent activity of spirit. Because of his idealistic tendency, Baur did not differentiate between historical and philosophical myths; only the philosophical myth was of interest to him.

Two points speak against Müller's suggestion: 1) in <u>Das Leben Jesu</u> Strauss seldom, if ever, designates a myth as philosophical and 2) there is no indication that the mythic played any role in his thinking prior to 1832. In his work on Strauss, Harris contends that Baur had no significant influence on the development of Strauss's mythic viewpoint. He points out that while Baur did lecture on mythology at Blaubeuren, his <u>Symbolik und Mythologie</u> was concerned almost exclusively with classical and non-biblical mythology. Baur himself was influenced by Creuzer and made no mention, as Strauss, however, did, of Eichhorn, Gabler, or Bauer.[50] Sandberger, on the other hand, maintains that Strauss first encountered the myth concept through Baur. However, Sandberger continues, this was not Baur's primary significance for Strauss; rather, it was through Baur's influence that Strauss developed into an historical critic.[51]

### 3. The "Mythic Principle"

It is Harris's contention that Strauss's "mythical principle" was quite distinct from the myth concept of Heyne's mythic school. Harris writes:

> Strauss's theory differs significantly from all previous mythical interpretations in that the mythical principle which he employed derived the Gospel from the Old Testament narratives by means of an unconscious mythologizing process.[52]

According to Harris, Strauss came to his mythic principle by way of four little-known writings.[53] Strauss refers to them all, particularly the third article mentioned by Harris.

The first was an article dealing with the first two chapters in Matthew and Luke. It was entitled "Beyträge zur Aufklärung über die beyden ersten Kapitel in Matthäus and Lucas," was signed E.F., and appeared in Magazin für Religionsphilosophie, Exegese, und Kirchengeschichte (1796). In a second article entitled "Ueber Offenbarung und Mythologie," which was published anonymously in 1799, the author, supposedly J.C.A. Grohmann, maintained that the historical Jesus was different from the Gospel Jesus. The idea of the Messiah was present before Jesus appeared, and Jesus was fashioned according to this idea.[54] This view was, to be sure, basic to Strauss's mythic interpretation.

In Harris's view, an anonymous article entitled "Die verschiedenen Rücksichten, in welchen und für welche der Biograph Jesu arbeiten kann," may have been, by virtue of its brevity and matter-of-factness, the argument that finally convinced Strauss that the mythic interpretation was the interpretative mode for the Gospels.[55] The 20 page article appeared in Kritisches Journal der neuesten theologischen Literatur (1816, V, No. 3). The author distinguished three viewpoints from which a biographer of Jesus could proceed: the purely historical viewpoint according to which the Gospel was either miraculous or natural history; the mythic viewpoint which left the material itself untouched and considered the Bible not history but holy legend;

the mixed viewpoint which was divided into the mythic-historical or the historical-mythic depending on whether myth or history prevailed.

When viewed as miraculous history, the literalness of the documents was asserted. The entire history, even where it was easily comprehensible, was considered a miracle, and the usual standard for credibility was rejected. Because of the consistency displayed in this position, respect could not be denied to its proponents.

Those who considered the Gospel natural history either eliminated the miraculous or sought to make the incomprehensible comprehensible through conjectures and additions. If executed consistently, this view became overburdened with arbitrariness in its attempts to extract the sacred and the divine. The author listed three features that made the scientific correctness of this view highly suspect: 1) a procedure in which documents were augmented by suspicions and speculations could hardly be considered an example of the historical method of investigation; 2) the effort to explain everything that was recorded as miraculous in natural terms was forced and flattered an age that demanded natural explanations for everything; 3) the proponents of this view who saw their method as a means of restoring dignity to the Gospels and increasing religiosity among the people were the victims of self-deception.

While not denying that an event might have been basic to most biblical narratives, the mythic view did not want to remove the real from its mythic guise. Proponents of this viewpoint considered it advisable to refrain from any judgment concerning the origin of individual myths since such attempts would always remain uncertain. Lending support to this view were the following: 1) the similarities between secular and Old Testament myths and New Testament history, e.g., the virgin birth (Hercules, Romulus, Alexander, Isaac, Simson, Samuel); 2) similarities between Jesus and the Old Testament prophets; with Elisha particularly Jesus shared many features (awakening of the dead, feeding the multitude, miraculous cures, crossing over water, blindness inflicted on those sent against them, host of invisible protectors); 3) the disappearance of numerous difficulties, e.g., time calculations and contradictions and/or omissions among different authors; 4) the removal from closer scrutiny of what was objectionable in the history of Jesus, e.g., the teachings of Jesus concerning possession by the devil that were referred to by theologians as accommodation to popular, current concepts; 5) the silence of secular writers.[56] This description of the mythic viewpoint anticipated essential elements in the criteria that Strauss later established to account for the sources of the biblical myth.

The mixed viewpoint had only recently gained in popularity. It originated with those theologians who did not want to give up history but could not be satisfied with its clear results. Their desire to unite both parties through this middle course was futile since the position would find favor neither with the rationalist nor the supranaturalist. Proponents of this view earned all the charges levelled against the naturalist, and since they also tried to allow for myth, they were also guilty of inconsistency, the worst charge that could be made against a scientific method. In addition, advocates of this view demonstrated the most extreme arbitrariness because purely subjective grounds determined what was myth and what was history.[57]

The fourth source mentioned by Harris and frequently appealed to by Strauss who faulted him only for limiting mythic intepretation to the period before Jesus' public appearance was Leonard Usteri, the author of "Beytrag zur Erklärung der Versuchungs-Geschichte" which appeared in <u>Theologischen Studien und Kritiken</u> (1832).[58] Although this article was confined to the temptation, Usteri did see parallels between Old Testament passages and the temptation story reported in the New Testament. According to Usteri myths were poetic productions that consisted of religious or philosophical ideas expressed in historical forms; their origin was no longer ascertainable. The myths about Jesus arose slowly and were written down some 30 years after His death, a period of time, Usteri suggested, which permitted the supernatural adornments of the historical basis to gain acceptance as history.[59]

Sandberger also sees Usteri as an important predecessor of Strauss. Not only Usteri's concept of myth but also the distinction between representation and concept connected with it and the radicalization of historical criticism through the speculative hermeneutics that resulted from this distinction anticipated essential elements in Strauss's Leben Jesu.[60]

In addition to Usteri, Sandberger also considers W. Vatke, whom Strauss met in Berlin and with whom he spent many an evening, the most important speculative theologian for Strauss. It is Sandberger's suggestion that Vatke encouraged Strauss to combine the myth concept, historical criticism, and speculative hermeneutics.[61] In his study on Strauss, Cromwell also suggests that Vatke had a significant influence on Strauss. In the lecture courses of Vatke, Cromwell maintains, Strauss heard his own view confirmed: the facts of history and the biblical representations did not correspond.[62]

### 4. Das Leben Jesu

#### a. Plans for Das Leben Jesu

In Literarischen Denkwürdigkeiten Strauss referred to Das Leben Jesu as an "inspired book; i.e., the author had absorbed the most powerful force of development in the science of theology at that time, and the book proceeded from this force."[63] Strauss planned this work while he was in Berlin in 1831-32. Before writing it, he intended to present the material in a series of lectures at the university in Tübingen. In response to Märklin's astonishment at the thought of lecturing on this topic, Strauss wrote:

> [I] am often quite sad that everything I would like to do in theology is such risky work. But

> I cannot change it; in some way, this material
> has to be produced out of me. . . . I first
> want to lecture, and only after that, do I want
> to write. In the meantime, let's commend it to
> God, Who in someway will open a door for
> something like this.[64]

Strauss described his plan for <u>Das Leben Jesu</u> in the above quoted letter to Märklin and in his <u>Streitschriften</u>.[65] The first part was to be a traditional account of Christian belief as it lives in the consciousness of the Church, objectively in its Gospels and subjectively in the individual believer. In the work itself, this part is merely peripheral.

The second part, the historical-critical section, became the actual body of the book. In this part all previous rationalistic and supernaturalistic attempts to interpret the Bible are refuted. Strauss first compares the various accounts of an event, points out inconsistencies, attempts to ascertain what was original in the accounts and what features in the reports could be considered historically accurate. He then considers the supernatural view, usually with Olshausen as its representative, and opposes it with arguments long employed by the rationalists; the rationalistic view is then considered, generally with Paulus as its representative, and arguments long employed by the supernaturalists are used against it. The absurdities and inconsistencies of these interpretative approaches and the futility of trying to harmonize different versions of the same event are emphasized. From this comparative investigation, Strauss draws the conclusion that the mythic view alone is possible, i.e., the event as narrated is unhistorical. His decision in favor of the mythic view is, thus, apogogic: after rejecting all other explanations for a fact, the necessity of the mythic explanation results.

Two principles support this conclusion: 1) external testimonies were not sufficient to assure eyewitness reports; any historical value ascribed to the reports was the result of later estimation; 2) prophecies from the Old Testament were applied by the Gospel writers to Jesus and to prophetic statements which He was supposed to have uttered.[66]

Strauss foresaw the results of historical criticism; his ultimate intention, however, was not the denial of the content of faith:

> In this way I would, in part, deny, in part, weaken the infinite content that faith has in this life in order to restore it in a higher way.[67]

In the third part, the dogmatic exposition, which Strauss saw as the easiest part, the positive elements of belief which had been destroyed were to be restored. In this section, which became, in Strauss's own words, a "mere supplement,"[68] Strauss develops his position concerning the union of the divine and human.

From the standpoint of the philosophy of religion, Strauss comments, nothing could be determined concerning the authenticity of the biblical narratives; what could be ascertained was whether what was reported had to have happened necessarily because of the truth of certain concepts. According to Strauss the necessity of the union of God and man in one person could not be maintained.[69] To do so was to confuse reality in general with a particular reality. Just as it was impossible to derive from the idea of beauty or virtue that one particular person was the highest and the sole perfect realization of this idea, so, too, was it impossible to derive from the idea of the human and divine that it was necessarily realized in Jesus. The reality of this idea, Strauss asserted, was realized in all of mankind, in the fullness of many examples.

b. Strauss's Concept of Myth

Strauss defines myth as the representation of an event or idea in an historical form but characterized by the pictorial and imaginative thought and expression of primitive ages.[70] His definition agrees with that of his predecessors. Strauss also retains the three classes of myth: the historical at the basis of which was a real event; the philosophical in which a thought, precept, or idea was presented in the guise of history; and the poetic which was a blend of the philosophical and historical so embellished by the poetic imagination that the original fact or idea was almost obscured. However, when Strauss specifically applies the myth concept to the Bible, his primary interest is the historical myth.

According to Strauss the pure evangelic myth had two sources: 1) the messianic ideas and expectations existing in the minds of the Jewish people prior to Jesus' appearance and independent of Him and 2) the particular impression left by the personal character, actions, and fate of Jesus.[71] The mythic conceptions gathered from these sources were seized with religious enthusiasm and woven around a definite individual fact to produce the historical myth found in the Bible. Strauss distinguishes between myth and legend or saga, the latter having its origin in the long course of oral tradition, but does not employ this distinction in his critical analysis.

The myth had two moments: 1) it was not history, and this afforded the negative criteria; 2) it was poetry from the spiritual tendency of a particular community, and this provided the positive criteria. The negative criteria consisted in the contradiction of the reported event with itself and with other events and its nonconformity to known psychological laws and the laws of causality and succession. Positive identification of a myth required that it be written in poetic form and that its content agree with certain ideas that seemed to be the product of preconceived opinions rather than of practical experience. In addition, if the context in which a particular narrative appeared had already been shown to have a connection with supernatural incidents, it was probable that the particular narrative itself would be mythic. To attain definite results a concurrence of several such indications was required.[72]

Because the borderline between myth and history was so narrow, two additional factors had to be considered. First, if two narratives excluded each other with respect to their content, only one could be historical; both, however, could be unhistorical. Historical accuracy could only be determined by agreement with some other well-authenticated testimony. Secondly, if particular parts of a narrative were credible in themselves but so intimately connected with the incredible that if the former were removed, the latter would lose all basis for credibility, the particular parts had to be considered mythic.[73]

Strauss's application of the myth concept was more consistent than that of his predecessors, for he left untouched no incident in the life of Jesus from the birth through the miracles and speeches to the death, resurrection, and second coming. He was more radical, for in addition to showing the absurdities that resulted from a literal interpretation, he also critically analyzed the rationalistic attempts that sought to maintain wherever possible at least a shred of history. Historical elements, however, were not totally eliminated by Strauss. Jesus remained an historical person; He grew up in Nazareth, was baptized by John, gathered disciples, traveled as a teacher in the Jewish countryside, opposed the Pharisees, invited man to the Kingdom of the Messiah, and was crucified. Strauss did not deny that Jesus was an exemplary man; that the Gospels contained excellent maxims pronounced by Him; that He gave the impression of being the Messiah and appropriated for Himself the Messianic role; that after His death, the opinion was formed among Christians, not from deception but from exaltation, that He arose. But that

Jesus was the incarnate God, that the dogmas espoused by the Christian Church concerning the person of Jesus were based on historical facts, this Strauss had to deny on the basis of historical criticism and on the basis of speculative philosophy.

Chapter Three

Critical Response to Das Leben Jesu

1.  Das Leben Jesu seen as Destructive Criticism

In general, Strauss's critics correctly saw Das Leben Jesu as the culmination of what had been going on in biblical exegesis for the previous 50 years and as the consistent result of one direction taken by speculative philosophy and theology. Rationalistic and naturalistic interpreters had rid the Bible of its supernatural elements and reduced the person of Christ to an exemplary teacher whose moral directives could be followed because they were rational. With this interpretation error in the Bible was explained by the theories of intentional deception or accommodation. The mythic view refuted these theories and was welcomed by its proponents as a means of restoring to the biblical authors and therewith to the Bible itself the dignity that had been lost.

The mythic mode of representation and style was seen as a necessary early stage in the development of reason and gradually as the universal, innate human mode of representing the divine. Application of the myth concept was at first restricted to the

Old Testament, but it soon became obvious that mythic-like elements were also contained in the New Testament. Once mythic elements were admitted in the birth narratives, the way was opened to extend application of the myth theory to all sections of the New Testament. But with this mode of interpretation, the truth of what was reported was no less diminished than in previous interpretative attempts, for as the amount of mythic material increased, the amount of historically true material proportionately decreased. In <u>Das Leben Jesu</u> Strauss summarized the results that had been achieved in biblical exegesis by mythic interpreters. Strauss then carried these results to their inevitable end: the Bible was the product of mythic imagination.

This result was seen as conditioned by Strauss's philosophical bias which was revealed in the dogmatic section of <u>Das Leben Jesu</u>. Here Strauss stated that the truth of an idea was realized not in an individual but in all of mankind.[74] The tendency of the age to generalize and spiritualize the particular and individual could not fail to have a negative effect when applied to the documents basic to Christian teaching. If truth was only in the idea, if the particularization of the idea was simply a necessary stage in the development of the idea that had to be cancelled if truth was to emerge in itself, then what Jesus claimed for Himself or what was claimed for Him by the first Christian community and all successive Christian communities was, at best, the inadequate form of the idea whose element of truth could only be revealed by philosophical thought.[75]

As a result of his historical critical study, Strauss pronounced the Bible the product of mythic imagination; the reconstruction that was intended to reestablish dogmatically what had been destroyed critically made humanity the subject of the predicates that had been assigned to Christ.[76] The result of either the historical or the dogmatic demonstration in itself would have been sufficient reason for contemporaries to label the work negative with respect to traditional Christian teaching. Because both demonstrations were mutually supportive in their negative conclusion, the entire investigation was considered negative in its fundamental tendency, and Strauss himself was unjustly accused of entertaining a prejudiced attitude toward his subject:

> An impartial criticism will never approach the investigation of a suspected untruth in a <u>merely</u> <u>negative</u> way; rather it will also have a <u>positive</u> attitude and will try to communicate the essential truth. Strauss's criticism, however, primarily has only a negative side; its <u>positive</u> side only wants to demonstrate that what was resolved in itself by the negative criticism was only fiction, a fiction now of the more unintentionally working saga, now of intentional poetry.[77]

To an extent, the critics of Strauss were correct in emphasizing the negativism of his work. Strauss did entertain doubts concerning the historical truth of what was reported in the Bible, and the results of his investigation certainly did not support traditional Christian beliefs.

However, Strauss did not consider the intended resolution a negative activity. Strauss conceived of his Leben Jesu as an attempt to put Christianity on a more solid basis both historically and dogmatically. What his critics saw as resolution aimed at destruction, Strauss saw as resolution aimed at elevation to a higher truth. When he wrote Das Leben Jesu, Strauss saw himself as both critic and believer. As a critic of the nineteenth century, he was filled with veneration for every religion, especially for the substance of Christianity:

> which he [the critic] perceives to be identical with the deepest philosophical truth; and hence, after having in the course of his criticism exhibited only the differences between his conviction and the historical belief of the Christian, he will feel urged to place that identity in a just light.[78]

It was not negativity per se nor the penchant for destruction that determined the outcome of Das Leben Jesu; rather the outcome resulted from the integrity of Strauss's historical sense as well as from his interpretation of the principles of Hegelian philosophy.

## 2. Dogmatic Assumptions Precluding Acceptance of the Mythic Viewpoint

For the critics who responded to Strauss in the journals being considered here, the way in which the Bible was to be considered was a genuine problem. The mixed viewpoint suggested by the anonymous author of "Die verschiedenen Rücksichten, in welchen und für welche der Biograph Jesu arbeiten kann" (v. above p.35-38) actually went beyond the definition of the author. For those theologians who did not want to give up history and yet could not accept the negative results to which historical criticism led, the Bible was not merely a combination of mythic and historical elements with no sound criteria to distinguish either precisely. The Bible was in part, myth, in part, saga, in part, moral instruction, in part, the product of inspiration and enthusiasm, in part, a finite vehicle for eternal truth; it was history, but what kind of history was it? Miraculous history? Natural history? Religious and moral history? Mythic history? A chapter in the historical development of an idea? A combination of two, three, all of these possibilities?

For the critics the Bible was history, but it was history with a qualification because the critics wanted the Bible to be two things: the history of the person Jesus, i.e., the historically true reproduction of the life of a concrete individual, and the history of the Lord and Founder of the absolute religion. Without the former, the dogmas of Christianity had no basis in history and had to forego the proofs for its claims which only history could provide; without the latter, Christianity was a religion among other religions whose truth could still be surpassed since the goal toward which all religion strove, the union of God and man, was not realized in its founder.

This confusion on the part of the critics is reflected in the dogmatic assumptions and the attempts to refute the presuppositions found operative in <u>Das Leben Jesu</u>. Its roots were twofold: 1) the equivocal attitude toward historical criticism when applied to a religious object in whose truth one believed and 2) the conscious task of firmly grounding Christianity as the absolute religion. In their attempts to allow for historical criticism--which they basically did not want to exclude because they realized that the truth of Christianity was not indifferent to the results of historical criticism--critics put restrictions on historical criticism in the form of dogmatic presuppositions which they saw as conditions or postures requisite to any historical investigation of the facts basic to Christian belief. The result was the transgression of the integrity of both the dogmatic and the historical-critical areas.

The fundamental presupposition of the more or less explicitly expressed dogmatic assumptions which were the basis for the objections raised against a purely historical approach to the Gospel narratives was the existence of a transcendent, personal God. From this resulted the insistence on the distinctiveness of the religious area vis-à-vis the areas of philosophy, history, and science and on the difference in the manner by which the truth of the ideas proclaimed in each area could be established. Essential features of this position were: the argument from sufficient cause, the assumption that because the Gospels were religious documents, fictitious elements were an impossibility (in effect, the reversal of a principle of the mythic view with respect to miracles), and an emphasis on the spiritual life that began with Jesus.

### a. J.C.F. Steudel

Because religion addressed not just one human faculty but the total person and because its truth was essentially of a moral and religious nature as distinct from an exclusively historical or philosophical nature, it was deemed a reasonable requirement that only one who was religiously disposed could undertake an historical investigation of an object whose import was primarily religious. If it was not absurd to demand of one judging colors that she/he not be color blind, was it any less absurd, Steudel asked, to demand of one judging of religious matters that she/he be pious?[79] At first glance the analogy--which would be considered appropriate by all the commentators treated here--sounds convincing. And if with this demand the critics had merely intended to emphasize that religious objects, like any other subjects of scientific investigation, should not be approached with preconceived negative opinions, the demand would be appropriate. But as the analogy suggests, sight was being ascribed to the believer and denied to the non-believer, an assumption that was itself based on presuppositions concerning the person of Jesus and the nature of the biblical documents.

For Steudel any investigation of the documents of Christianity had to include the two aspects that belonged to the essence of Christianity, viz., the historical and the religious. The historical approach consisted in highlighting the agreement of the documents with the spirit, content, and characteristics of Christianity; it had to proceed from the <u>historical</u> presupposition that it was dealing with the life of one who was what he said he was and from whom visible effects still proceeded. The religious element consisted in receptivity to the new life proceeding from Christ.[80]

### b. Carl F. Stäudlin

According to Stäudlin the mind and heart of Jesus was filled by and with the divine. As a result, any actions or words that were attributed to Him did not merely have historical importance but incorporated absolute, eternal truths; they were revelation. To be sure, Jesus availed Himself of the language, terminology, and ideas current at that time, and to the extent that historical criticism confined itself to explaining the intended sense of a passage, it was useful in biblical exegesis. But because Jesus was divinely endowed, such explanations could not be considered equivalent to giving an account of the moral and religious content of the passage in question. Historical criticism, Stäudlin maintained, had to be complemented by religious, moral, and philosophical interpretations.[81]

Stäudlin's insistence on an area within which historical criticism might legitimately work was in and of itself a correct scientific distinction. Nor could there by any objection to complementing historical interpretation with other interpretative modes. However, the ambivalence of Stäudlin's position toward historical criticism, which was already suggested by his concept of Jesus as one whose mind and heart were filled by God, becomes more evident when further statements made by him are taken into account.

Stäudlin suggested that historical exegetes began to go astray when they assumed that what was found through historical investigation was only something historical.[82] He recognized that this assumption on the part of historical critics belonged to the essence of the undertaking, but his recognition could only be half-hearted because for Stäudlin the Bible was not only history but also instruction. The Books of the Bible were written partly as documents, partly as the explanation and application of divine revelation in acts and in words; they were written with intense religious and moral feeling and contained penetrating glances into human and divine nature. In addition, the Gospels themselves gave one to understand that not even Jesus' own followers always understood the full sense of what He was saying, that full understanding would only be given to them after His death under the guidance of the Holy Spirit.[83]

For Stäudlin the divinity of Christ and the inspired nature of the Gospels were givens. Consequently, for him only historical investigations that proceeded from these facts and whose results were in harmony with them were appropriate. Historical criticism, in other words, was acceptable only if it agreed to accept assumptions whose content lay outside its principles of investigation and verification.

### c. Ernst Friedrich Gelpke

E.F. Gelpke argued that both the general principles of historical research as well as indications in the Gospels themselves demanded that considerations other than those of the purely historical standpoint took priority in evaluating the content of the Gospels. This argument, Gelpke stated, rested on the A PRIORI ground that the Gospels were not history per se, were not the history of religion, but were religious history. As such, the Bible envisaged only the particular religious needs of individuals and arranged the historical material according to these needs; it was not intended to be a completely true historical picture of a definite religious phenomenon or period. What the Gospels contained was the history of the founder of Christianity as conceived by His first inspired pupils and followers, who wanted to present a picture of Him that conveyed their enthusiasm and awakened similar enthusiasm in others. Consequently, only the facts that most deeply affected religious consciousness were recorded.[84]

Gelpke also acknowledged that the significance of the Gospels went beyond this definition. Because they contained the words and deeds of the Founder of Christianity, the Gospels, in addition to being religious history, were also the history of the primitive Church, and, as such, they were the source of belief, the norm for all Christian thinking and acting. Could the Church be satisfied with a history to which the purely historical standpoint could not be applied?[85]

Gelpke's view on the nature of the Gospel permitted him to answer this question in the affirmative. The Gospels, Gelpke stated, were written to satisfy the need of the primitive community for a history not of Jesus but of the Founder and Lord of the Church. And they continued to satisfy this same need. It was this subjective need and its satisfaction through the Gospels that provided the concrete link of continuity between past and present. This subjective element, however, did not prevent the Gospels from being historical documents. What provided assurance that facts were basic to the Gospels was the principle of sufficient cause: a history without a Christ, a history filled with unparalled devotion and enthusiasm for an individual was inconceivable without such an individual.[86]

Implicit in Gelpke's entire argument was the conviction that ultimately historical truth had no bearing on religious truth. For Gelpke the Gospels would retain their value even if their entire content were pronounced myth, i.e., they would remain a perfect record of subjective religious consciousness. In this lay the historical value of the Gospels. But Gelpke was not unaware of the consequences that would result for the claims to the truth of Christian dogma if the Gospels were only to be considered religious history. Thus his introduction of the principle of sufficient cause: the subjective religious needs were satisfied because Christ truly existed. The flaw in this was that the intended transition to the historical area was not accomplished: the cause, like the effects, remained in the area of the religious, for the cause was not the historical Jesus but the Christ of Christian belief, or, in Gelpke's words, the Founder and Lord of the Christian Church. For Gelpke historical criticism had to proceed from the presupposition that Christ was Who He said He was, i.e., for Gelpke the historically verifiable subjective need for the Lord of the Church provided the necessary proof that the Lord of the Church had to exist. Gelpke, thus, brought into the historical area presuppositions appropriate only to the religious area.

### d. Johann Tobias Beck

While Beck respected Strauss's request that criticism of his <u>Leben Jesu</u> be withheld until the publication of the second part, he, nonetheless, felt it could be to the advantage of the second part if certain points were discussed prior to its appearance. He, therefore, asked what he considered to be the fundamenal question in regard to Strauss's work: was the mythic view rooted in a standpoint that was compatible with the spirit that flowed from the primitive Christian community?[87] This question itself was grounded in a sound hermeneutic principle: in any attempt at an historical description of Christianity, the responsibility to reproduce the original in a true image had to be assumed. This responsibility was abdicated if the Gospels were approached with an A PRIORI assumption concerning the spirit and teaching of Christ and if the procedure aimed at producing a history of Christ that coincided with this assumption. Beck leveled this charge against Strauss, but if it applied to Strauss, it was no less applicable to Beck. For Beck was convinced that the very spirit of Christianity per se precluded the inclusion of purely fictional elements. The safeguard against the inclusion of such elements and against any deficiencies attributable to imperfect human nature was the witness of the Spirit: "Christianity insists that its Paraclete co-exists only with the most exact truth and that no human fiction can arise under its seal."[88]

The phrasing of Beck's question itself betrayed an unscientific posture. Not only did Beck presuppose an historical basis for the religious spirit emanating from the Gospels--a presupposition based on religious belief in the witness of the Spirit-- but he also required that the investigator approach the subject to be investigated with a standpoint that had to be in harmony with this spirit, i.e., Beck was not merely advocating openness and receptivity to the object of investigation but was requiring a viewpoint that automatically conditioned the results.

### e. Carl Ullmann

According to Ullmann there was an historical ground for what was reported in the Gospels, but this ground was not historical in the generally accepted sense because the history of the founding of a religion by its very nature had to have a different character from usual history. When a religion originated, a twofold relationship occurred. First, as a new spiritual creation, the formation of a religion led back to divine causality: the extraordinary features that accompanied it referred to the inexplicable but also to God. Secondly, a religious creation with respect to its original founding among humankind was conceivable only in a state of inspiration; in such a state, criticism and historical pragmatism receded and were replaced by the feeling of devotion and love and the interest for ideas, for the inner meaning of the historical. Consequently, if it was to be assessed according to its true nature, the history of the founding of a religion had to be treated accordingly, i.e., it had to be received in the same spirit in which it was given.[89]

As an object worthy of belief, the religious truth contained in the Bible could be known by its moral and religious significance and by the fact that it was the representation of an idea. By virtue of the latter the Bible could be designated "eternal history."[90] When viewed as "eternal history," the question of the reality of the recorded events became insignificant in the evaluation of the biblical narratives: they were sublime poetry. But Christianity claimed to be more than the beauty and representation of an idea; it claimed truth and reality. Ullmann readily admitted that historical truth could not be ascribed to the Gospels simply because they had religious significance.[91] To have historical truth, religious truth had to fulfill three conditions: 1) obvious divine purposiveness: 2) inextinguishable connection with other incontestable and morally imperative truths and facts; 3) historical effects of a truly salutary nature.

Christianity satisfied all three requirements: 1) the transformation of mankind that was to be mediated only in this way justified the extraordinary; 2) its Founder was a Person of unique moral and spiritual greatness, Whose teaching contained inner truth and goodness; 3) it appeared as a link in the whole, corresponding to the given conditions of every age and to the higher nature of the Redeemer. While an absolutely demonstrable proof was not possible, the most well-founded justification for belief in the truth of biblical history existed: the teaching contained in it was so great and unique, the image portrayed was so powerful and individual, the miraculous and extraordinary were so guaranteed by continuous and continuing efficaciousness that they had to be traced back to a concrete historical person. The Bible, Ullmann concluded, was historically grounded and the structure of Christianity had a sure foundation: the person of Jesus.[92]

Ullmann's apologetics revolves around two central points: 1) the distinctiveness of the truth of religious ideas which cannot be demonstrated logically or empirically but rather require belief with its component elements of piety and moral trust and 2) the argument of sufficient cause, i.e., the redeeming and liberating effects proceeding from Christianity became incomprehensible if the cause for these effects was not the historical figure of Jesus as portrayed in the Gospels. The uniqueness of the effects necessarily referred back to a unique individual; a fact, viz., the teaching and life of Christ had to be basic to the idea of salvation. In developing these points, Ullmann presented variations of arguments already discussed: the special nature of religious documents vis-à-vis history, the subordination of historical interest to religious needs, the state of moral and religious inspiration present at the time of composition--a state that the investigator had to approximate--and the purity of the religious and moral spirit that emanated from the Gospels.

Ullmann recognized both the dogmatic and the subjective nature of these arguments and knew that he was working from an epistemological principle according to which the nature of religion belonged more to the area of feeling than to reason. He was, furthermore, aware that this principle had a significant effect on how the truth claims of Christianity were approached. Therefore, he posited the conditions which had to be fulfilled if historical truth was to be assigned to religious truth. The conditions, however, were themselves conditioned by dogmatic presuppositions: it was decreed by God that man be reconciled to Him through the life and death of the Redeemer. Since man now knew he was saved, this Redeemer must have lived.

## f. Summary

The critics considered above excluded the documents of the Christian religion from any interpretation that was of a purely historical nature because they were convinced of the uniqueness of religion in general and of Christianity in particular. It was on the basis of this conviction that they attempted to check any interpretation which threatened to treat the Gospels merely as another piece of literature. The similarity between the biblical narratives and the religious or secular literature of other ancient peoples, they asserted, was cancelled by the salutary efficaciousness and the purity of the moral and religious spirit that proceeded from the Christian religion. Ultimately, it was this uniqueness of Christianity that was to provide the irrefutable argument for the historical nature of Christianity. But the claim to uniqueness, if intended to refute the results of Strauss's investigation, became impotent because Strauss's critics confused what Strauss succeeded in keeping distinct.

By its very nature, historical criticism is the critical study of human activity as it manifests itself in concrete documents, one of which is the written record. From the perspective of historical criticism, the Bible can only be viewed as a humanly composed record which has the purpose of serving a particular religious end. As part of its investigation, historical criticism can legitimately compare the Bible with other religious documents, pointing out shared literary features and any elements that would appear to be unique. If the findings of such a comparative literary criticism result in calling into question the historical nature of the facts supposed to be basic to the document under investigation, historical criticism has to be free to pronounce this result. Strauss was, therefore, within his right to deny historical truth, i.e., facticity, to the biblical narratives.

Strauss's critics could not, or would not, grant to historical criticism such a carte blanche position vis-à-vis the Bible. Their reluctance to do so can be explained by their insistence on the special nature of the Bible. For Strauss, however, the Gospel as the product of human activity had no claims to such special treatment; for him any distinction between sacred and secular literature was contrary to the fundamental presupposition of historical criticism:

> One word expresses the presupposition of historical criticism: the essential similarity of everything that happened.[93]

In the historical section Strauss was considering the Bible solely as a piece of religious literature; his critics, however, wanted to incorporate into historical criticism religious convictions as historical facts, e.g., the witness of the spirit, the inspired nature of the Gospels, the divinity of the historical person of Jesus. But just as historical criticism oversteps its bounds when from the non-facticity of the Bible it concludes that no truth can be ascribed to it, so, too, does faith overstep its bounds when it tries to establish historical facts from within its own resources. If facticity is not the same as truth, neither are dogmatic presuppositions historical facts. Strauss's work was considered absolutely free of any dogmatic presuppositions. While his critics viewed this as a fault, Strauss was correct in seeing such "internal liberation of the feelings and intellect from certain religious and dogmatical presuppositions"[94] as an essential requirement in the area of criticism. It is precisely because the proclaimed uniqueness of Christianity rested on dogmatic and religious grounds and not on historical grounds that it had no bearing on the historical approach to the Gospels.

In addition to resting on dogmatic and religious grounds, the claim to uniqueness was also supported by the appeal to the continuous and continuing efficaciousness of Christianity. Such efficaciousness, however, could be explained by the human need for credulity, i.e., as a purely subjective phenomenon. Thus, from this standpoint also no sufficient ground was offered for reestablishing the historical truth of the Gospels that was called into question by Strauss's critique.

### 3. Speculative and Empirical Presuppositions Found Operative in Strauss

In the introduction to volume one of the first edition of <u>Das Leben Jesu</u>, Strauss admits to having obtained freedom from certain religious and dogmatic presuppositions by means of philosophical studies.[95] The importance he attached to this freedom as an essential requirement in scientific investigation finds its most decisive expression in the Streitschriften where admittedly it assumes a defensive tone:

> In scientific matters, spirit acts freely; thus it should also lift its head in candor and not lower it submissively. Not the sacred but only truth exists immediately for science. Truth, however, does not demand the cloud of incense of devotion but the clarity of thought and speech. Furthermore, spirit knows no danger whenever it is conscious of following the track of truth; rather, it is completely calm about the goal to which it is being led, confident that it will be the best. The devotional, anxious manner in matters of science can only serve to make thought shy and confused, to corrupt it with foreign considerations. Instead of leading thought forward to the truth, it leads it backwards in a circle to that point where prejudice long stood and wishes to be left.[96]

For Strauss the significance of this freedom lay not so much in the negative aspect suggested by his critics but rather in the positive aspect of clearing the path for the pursuit of truth.

While his critics had no problem in granting Strauss freedom from religious-dogmatic presuppositions, the question of philosophical presuppositions was a totally different matter. Ullmann found in Das Leben Jesu every presupposition of a certain tendency of modern culture and of a definite philosophical school.[97] Alexander Schweizer accused Strauss of bringing to his exegesis and critique the views of a system which exerted a direct influence on his position.[98] Daniel Schenkel found the source of Strauss's view in the abstract dialectic view of God

and the world espoused by the most recent philosophy. This view
assumed its necessary position in contemporary history as the
apex of modern consciousness but was irreconcilable with the fundamental truths of Christianity.[99] According to Friedrich
Vorländer the fundamental presuppositions of Strauss's critique
were those of the Hegelian system. The results of Strauss's critical examination, Vorländer continued, demonstrated the conflict
of this system with the positive reality of Christianity. And
this conflict was presented:

> with clear consciousness...,...with ruthless,
> scientific consistency.... What is now explicit,
> now implicit, in Hegel's philosophy of religion,
> viz., that Christ as the redeeming Son of God is
> the product of the community, of the Church, but
> not an actual, divine fact...this is what Strauss
> bluntly teaches and seeks to convey in his
> criticism.[100]

Vorländer's judgment was pronounced even more forcefully by
Julius Müller who saw Strauss's work as: "the product of a definite fanaticism in speculation."[101] With Strauss, Müller continued, the Hegelian school made a decisive break with
Christianity: Christianity ceased being revelation and was
degraded to the dignity of a mythology so that the progress of
speculative philosophy would not be impeded.[102] Strauss affirmed
the connection between Hegel's philosophy and *Das Leben Jesu*. He
writes: "From its origin my criticism of the life of Jesus was
intimately connected with Hegelian philosophy."[103] For Strauss
the most important point in this system was the distinction between representation and concept. When he first encountered this

distinction in his university years, he thought that it reconciled in the most satisfying way respect for the biblical documents and Church dogmas with freedom of thought toward the same. The relationship between the concept and the historical components of the Bible became the most important question for Strauss:

> [D]id the historical nature belong to the content which was the same for representation and concept and did it also require recognition by the latter or could it be relegated to mere form in consequence of which conceptual thought was not bound to it?[104]

Thus, according to Strauss himself, it was the distinction between representation and concept and the question as to the extent to which the concept was bound to the historical elements of a given content that determined his approach to the Gospels.

The presuppositions that the critics found operative in Strauss were of two kinds: speculative and empirical. The speculative principles concerning the nature of religion, the distinction between concept and representation, and the realization of the idea not in one individual but in mankind as a whole unquestionably resulted from Strauss's study of Hegelian philosophy. The rejection of the miraculous as a violation of the principle of causality was more a scientific principle. However, it was not unrelated to philosophical thought. In rationalistic thought causality as a principle of reason permitted no exception; Strauss's inclination to view the miraculous as unhistorical and to demand the most convincing kind of supporting testimony for it could, thus, be seen as part of the rationalistic legacy inherited by him. At the same time, the denial of the miraculous was part of any world view that excluded the possibility of a personal God and, therewith, of the supernatural in general.

The presence of these presuppositions in <u>Das Leben Jesu</u> is evident. The nature of their actual influence on the procedure and the results, however, was not as simple as the critics implied. While the speculative principles had a definite bearing on the dogmatic section, their role in the historical-critical section is more subtle. And while the empirical presupposition is certainly obvious in the historical-critical section, its application is not as arbitrary as the critics suggest. The critics considered all four presuppositions false. Accordingly, their critique of these presuppositions must be considered both with respect to their interpretation of the role of these presuppositions in <u>Das Leben Jesu</u> and with respect to the impact of their own assumptions on the arguments used to reject the conclusions of Strauss.

a. Concept of Religion

Strauss's concept of the essence of religion reflected his understanding of Hegelian philosophy. For him the essence of religion was the idea of the union of God and man. On the level of belief, knowledge of this idea assumed the form of representation and on that of speculation, the form of the concept. It was on the basis of this distinction that Strauss was able to submit biblical history to a critical examination in the conviction that if any of its components proved to be unhistorical, this would have no damaging effect on the truth of religion itself; what was essential in religion would remain and would be raised from the form of representation to that of the concept. In investigating the historical truth or non-truth of the Gospel, Strauss was trying to determine both the extent to which historical truth was necessary to the dogmas of Christian faith and the extent to which the recorded events were merely the concretization of an idea which as the form of representational thought could safely be ignored by conceptual thought.

Kern and Ullmann saw Strauss as the proponent of a one-sided position. By having grasped religious truth solely as a correct and complete development of the concept of God, Ullmann maintained, Strauss had failed to take cognizance of what had been achieved by modern theology which had demonstrated that the essence of religion was not knowledge, that Christianity was not originally teaching and doctrine. There was, admittedly, a side of religion that was turned toward knowledge, viz., teaching; this area belonged to the sphere of theology and was capable of unending development and perfectibility. But this was only one aspect of religion. Religion itself was life, consciousness, the unique state of affection of the entire spirit. In its innermost being, religion was the conscious reference of the entire life of an individual to God.[105] Only by proceeding from the presupposition that the idea was God and God was the idea, Kern observed, was it possible for Strauss to grasp God as caught up in an endless process that repeated itself. God was not merely an idea; the idea was not God. God was the personal God Who most perfectly revealed Himself in the person of Jesus.[106].

These explicit references to Strauss's concept of religion were implied by other critics in their discussion of Strauss's Christology. Fundamental to their argument was a rejection of the Straussian concept of religion in favor of the more comprehensive concept of religion presented by Schleiermacher. Inherent to their argument is belief in a personal, transcendent God, the possibility of which was totally ignored by Strauss.

b. Representation and Concept

The irreconcilability of Hegelian philosophy with the fundamental truths of Christianity, the conflict of this system with the positive reality of Christianity, to which Schenkel, Vorländer, and Müller referred, was ultimately rooted in the distinction between concept and representation. This distinction had a direct effect on the historical area, and, to the extent that religion is an historical phenomenon, on the religious area as well.

Strauss's concept of myth was seen either as a necessary consequence of Hegel's system or as an hypothesis that harmonized with the principles of Hegel's philosophy of religion and philosophy of history. While there were adherents of Hegel's system, e.g., Marheineke, Braniss, and Weisse, who sought to demonstrate the compatibility of Hegel's philosophy with Christianity, there were also proponents of the system whose application of Hegelian principles resulted in conclusions that were in opposition to the traditional teachings of the Church. The term Older Hegelian School was coined for the former group; members of the latter constituted the Younger Hegelian School.

The primary advantage that the Younger School was thought to have had over the Older School lay not so much in a more correct understanding or a more fundamental interpretation of Hegel, but rather in the insight its members achieved with respect to the untenability of the position of philosophy in relation to the Church, the state, and world-historical spiritual development assumed by Hegel and retained by his older disciples. Philosophy, it was asserted, could no more boast of having attained its goal than it could ascribe to the forms of Church and state the attainment of their respective goals. Philosophy had to retain for itself and for Church and state the right to free criticism and unlimited progress. The work of Strauss, who, together with Ludwig Feuerbach and A. Ruge,[107] was celebrated by many of the Younger Hegelians as one of the leading figures of the age, was viewed as a source of encouragement for those who quietly or by means of an ambiguous language already perceived themselves in opposition to the older faction and the political and ecclesiastic teachings with which this faction was linked.[108]

For reasons compatible with his principles of philosophizing, Hegel was somewhat apprehensive about historical criticism; he could find no principle of immanent scientific decision and certainty for it. The content of history itself, however, was of significance to him, and he could not consider its surrender to critical doubt a matter of indifference or of scientific advantage. In keeping with his principle on the relationship between representation and concept, Hegel considered belief in the factual truth of the content of both secular and sacred history a necessary transitional point to philosophical knowledge. For the great majority, it was a necessary surrogate for philosophical knowledge, but even for the philosophically initiated, it was the substantive background for true thought and knowledge. However, the content of history remained the content of conceptual thought and knowledge. It was for this reason that history was without an immanent criterion for the truth and non-truth of its elements.[109]

This in part accounts for the ambiguity in Hegel's thought with respect to the historical Jesus and the Christ of faith, an ambiguity which, in turn, explains why adherents of the system could either affirm or deny the reconcilability of the system with the teachings of Christianity. According to the principles of Hegel's philosophy, the process of spiritual religious development which for Hegel had its decisive turning point in the origin of Christianity was a process of the formation of religious representations which contained the truth of speculative thought in an inadequate form. In the <u>Lectures on the Philosophy of Religion</u>, Hegel seemed to suggest that the genesis of Christian representations occurred after Christ's death; that the life and deeds of Christ contained only the historical precondition for the process of the conversion of divine-human self-consciousness; that the process itself, however, proceeded not in the spirit of the person Jesus but in the spirit of His disciples. Since the significance of the historical Christ seemed to be degraded in favor of the ideas which were to be formed in the spirit of the community, the designation of Christ as the bearer of the divine did become difficult to understand. What Hegel seemed to be suggesting was that traces of the historical Christ were to be considered as something indifferent or uncertain, whereas the image of Christ born out of the sense of the community in free creative activity should be valued.

Strauss, Weisse suggested, was influenced by Hegel's distinction between representation and concept and by his view of history and religion in a twofold way. First, for Strauss the criteria of scientific truth and certainty fell exclusively to the element of pure thought immediately and without the addition of intuition and representation. Whatever significance Hegel may have attributed to the element of representation with respect to its content was not heeded by Strauss. Rather, Strauss saw it as self-evident that representation dealt with particularity which could only be communicated by representation and not by pure thought; consequently, substantial religious and religious-philosophical thought could not be achieved. It was on this basis that Strauss took that historical moment in which such particularity was given to Christian belief and exposed it to a searching criticism of the understanding which dealt with finitudes and externalities. Secondly, Strauss's treatment of history was conditioned by his understanding of the relationship between the representation and its content to conceptual thinking. According to Strauss the moment of representation which belonged to historical truth as such and to religious truth to the extent that it formed itself into historical facts was indefinite; any attempt to delimit it scientifically reverted automatically to the reciprocal dialectic negation of its moment by virtue of the contradictions inherent in representation.

On the basis of his conviction that Hegel's philosophy could be reconciled with Christian teachings, Weisse pronounced Strauss's work a deviation from the spirit of Hegel's system. Nonetheless, he affirmed that it was a justifiable undertaking within the Hegelian system, for the relationship between concept and representation was incontestably grounded in the principles of Hegelian philosophy. But whereas for Hegel the elements of feeling and sensuality gave the representation a function independent of the concept, in Strauss the representation was only the temporary form of the concept which was destined to be resolved into the latter.[110]

Of the critics considered here, Weisse was the only one who attempted to explain in some detail the nature of the presupposition concerning the relationship between concept and representation that was operative in Das Leben Jesu. And yet in the Streitschriften Strauss himself had explicitly indicated the importance of precisely this distinction for his work on the New Testament. Weisse's intention, to be sure, was not to vindicate Strauss's application of this principle but to show that while it was legitimate within the context of Hegelian philosophy, it was incommensurable with the spirit of Hegel's philosophy. Weisse's assessment of Strauss's understanding of the Hegelian principle was correct and at least hinted at the specific way in which Strauss's concept of myth may have been influenced by Hegelian philosophy.

The historical-critical section of Das Leben Jesu was not concerned with a philosophical explanation for the origin of myths in general but rather with the historical process by which the biblical myths arose. In its execution, therefore, it is essentially free of specifically speculative presuppositions. Nonetheless, it is true that in 1835 Strauss saw the myth in Hegelian terms as one form for the realization of the idea. The distinction between representation and concept gave Strauss the freedom to apply historical criticism to the Bible. For while Strauss may have adopted, as he himself indicated in the genesis of the mythic interpretation, the mythic concept from the mythic school, the myth concept can also be seen as an implication of the Hegelian distinction between representation and concept.

For Strauss representation and myth became two different terms for the same thing; they differed only to the extent that representation as a systematic concept came from philosophy of religion, while the word "myth" as an historical concept came from biblical exegesis. For Strauss the mode of representation for primitive man was mythical; by representation Strauss understood the primitive stage of the enlightened concept. The representations used by man to express the contradictions that were perceived were seen by Strauss as indicative of a lower stage in the ability to think.[111] In so understanding the differentiation between representation and concept, Strauss, as Weisse pointed out, limited Hegel's theory, leaving out the elements of feeling and sensuality which in Hegel's system gave the representation a function independent of the concept. In Strauss the relationship between representation and concept was essentially non-dialectic since the representation was merely the temporary form of the concept which was destined to be resolved in the latter. As a result of his encounter with mythic interpreters, Strauss identified his understanding of representation with myth: for Strauss myth was the historical concretization of representation. What enabled Strauss to join speculative philosophy and historical criticism was, thus, his concept of representation: since the representation as the primitive level of thought was to be resolved into the concept, the myth as the historical concretization of this representation had to be destroyed.[112] Once Strauss established through historical criticism that the biblical reports were mythic, i.e., unhistorical,[113] he was then free to determine through speculative philosophy the necessity of the realization of the idea in one concrete individual. Thus, it is only within this context that the assertions of critics like Ullmann, Schweizer, and Vorländer, to the effect that the historical-critical section of <u>Das Leben Jesu</u> was ultimately conditioned either implicitly or explicitly by speculative presuppositions can be considered correct. Despite the significance of this presupposition, the critics emphasized the presuppositions connected with the problem of the archetype and the problem of development. According to them it was these presuppositions that predetermined the outcome of the historical-critical section.

c. Problem of the Archetype

That Christology came to occupy a central position in the conflict between Christian dogma and Hegelian philosophy was not surprising, for here the individual, the immediate object of intuition or representation, sought universal validity. In his speculative reconstruction, Strauss proceeded from the idea of the necessary unity of human and divine nature. As essential as this unity was for him, so unthinkable was it that it could be present in an individual in an exclusive way. Strauss sought to avoid the Kantian standpoint according to which idea and reality were separate and the ideal became an empty ought by affirming the reality of the idea in all of humankind and denying only its exclusive realization in one individual.

Strauss's contemporaries correctly identified the two principles basic to Strauss's Christology: 1) it was not the manner of the idea to realize itself in one individual but in the totality of individuals, in the species, and 2) the first one in a developmental series could not simultaneously be the greatest. While relative truth could be ascribed to these principles, absolute truth was denied them, and their application to the founder of Christianity was contested by the critics. Closely associated with the problem of the archetype and that of development was the question of the sinlessness of Jesus.

The rejection of the speculative principles that were fundamental to Strauss's attempt at a speculative reconstruction of Christology reflected the intention of the critics to defend the predicates that the Church has always ascribed to Christ as the God-man. The attempts to retain for Christ His unique position among men were supported by principles adopted and/or adapted from Schleiermacher's theology, by insisting on the reality of sin and its consequence for moral life, and by explaining Strauss's position as a consequence of his pantheistic tendency. Like Strauss, his critics also proceeded from the standpoint of idealism: whereas for Strauss humanity was the realization of the idea of the necessary unity of human and divine nature, for the critics Christ was this realization. In arguing for the truth of the latter, the critics were also defending Christianity as the absolute religion.

Strauss himself was of the opinion that at the time of Christ a religion arose which in some way was absolute, i.e., perfect and complete.[114] On the basis of his philosophical presuppositions, this absoluteness of Christianity had to be understood in terms of the dawning in human consciousness of the highest religious idea. Christ's role in this process was substantially diminished by Strauss; at best He could be considered a necessary impetus in initiating the process. For his critics the absoluteness of Christianity rested on totally different presuppositions.

The historical appearance of the idea in a single individual, Schweizer asserted, was the point towards which historical religions had been striving. Historical religions, he explained, were never formed or furthered through the joint contribution of many but through the mediation of prophetic individuals to receptive circles. This process found its completion in Christianity: a founder of the true universal Church who ruled all and whose religious life was to be infused into all so that he might live in all. This founder was to be the one in whom religious life that proceeded from self-consciousness and feeling most perfectly attained concrete existence. What was being asserted in the religious area, Schweizer maintained, was in agreement with the general principle according to which everything that was connected with an individual was best attained by an individual. History, Schweizer concluded, supported a position totally opposed to that of Strauss: the degree of determinateness with which the religious qualities of the founder of a religion could be established was simultaneously the standard of excellence of a religion and vice versa.[115]

Schweizer, who acknowledged the influence of Schleiermacher's theology and philosophy on his own thought, argued, accordingly, from a Schleiermacherian context. For him the religious area was an area in which a course of life was founded only through inspired intuition and the revealed indwelling of God. Schweizer did not attempt to refute Strauss's presuppositions; he merely argued from presuppositions concerning the nature of religion and the role of the individual in religious life that were fundamentally other than those of Strauss. Schweizer, however, tread on common ground with Strauss with his assertion concerning the relationship between the religious qualities of the founder of a religion and the eminence of the religion associated with him. Strauss would grant Schweizer this relationship, and to the extent that Christ was instrumental in awakening humankind to the consciousness of its union with God, Strauss would be inclined to grant Him an elevated position among the founders of religions. But this agreement would not cancel the fundamental difference between Strauss and Schweizer because Schweizer's argument did not address itself to the historical question considered by Strauss in the historical-critical section of <u>Das Leben Jesu</u>, i.e., Schweizer simply assumed that what was recorded was fact. In his investigation of Scripture, Strauss was attempting to ascertain just what religious qualities could be attributed to the man Jesus; for Schweizer the ascertainment of these qualities was primarily a speculative problem, and historical criticism had only to demonstrate that the image of the Founder of Christianity as recorded in the Gospels did, indeed, have these qualities.

Like Schweizer, Ullmann and Vorländer also argued that the absoluteness of Christianity was the guarantee that its founder had to be an individual who embodied religious and moral perfection. The idea of the unity of God and man, a trace of divine consciousness, ran through all peoples and ages and aimed at one central point. This idea found its historical perfection in Christ, the Son of God and of man. The absolute religion could only be founded when an individual bearing the creative fullness of divine life was really there. In addition, Ullmann suggested that Strauss was proceeding from an incorrect interpretation of Christian doctrine when he asserted that it was contrary to the idea to pour itself out in all its fullness in one individual to the exclusion of all others. In favoring one individual, Ullmann explained, God did not forget humankind; the principle of new life was given to one individual not for his own sake but for all who were receptive to it through him.[116]

For the critics the sinlessness of its founder was an indispensable requirement of the absolute religion. According to Strauss, however, any sameness that was claimed for Jesus' human nature and human nature in general was cancelled when sinlessness, defined as the impossibility of sinning, was posited of Him. Because sinlessness, understood not as the ability not to sin but the impossibility of sinning at all, contradicted human freedom, Strauss considered it irreconcilable with human nature.[117] Therefore, if Jesus was truly human, sinlessness could not be postulated of Him, i.e., Jesus could not be the archetype. However, by considering the unity with God as immanent in man, Strauss, in effect, posited the idea of the human as the subject of the predicates that Christianity gave to Christ, i.e., what he denied to any one individual, Strauss ascribed to the species as a whole. To demonstrate the inconsistency in Strauss's thought both with respect to the concept of absolute religion and with respect to the realization of the idea in the species, speculative demonstrations for the necessity of a sinless founder of the absolute religion were developed.

Kern argued that the necessity to sin did not belong to human nature per se but only to its temporal development up to that point in time when creation was perfected in one individual: Christ was this perfection because He lived that state to which humankind was destined to be raised. Christ's sinlessness, therefore, did not contradict human essence but was the realization of human essence. Kern defined the human essence as personality in which free, self-conscious subjectivity was perfectly determined by the being of God in the person: the being of God had become one with the human being in the form of God-consciousness. If there was a temporal development preceding the perfection of creation in which human personality did not correspond to this idea of humankind, which was first posited as a disposition through whose unfolding the idea was to be realized, and if creation had to be perfected in time because what was eternally grounded in the idea also had to appear in time, then it was necessary that in history that moment occurred when this perfection and the raising of personality into the unity with the idea began: one person had to appear in whom the idea was presented purely and completely so that all others might be raised to the perfection of creation and the true concept of the human.

Christ's sinlessness, consequently, could not be subsumed under the category of miracle since the perfection being posited of Him belonged essentially to the concept of the human. With respect to the development of God-consciousness, finite conditions demanded only that it be constant, not that it be burdened by sin; the possibility of a God-consciousness in which real harmony in the relationship between it and other functions of spiritual life took place was not excluded. If sinlessness was accepted as belonging to the concept of the human, if there was a human archetype with which the consciousness of its realization was given, then, Kern concluded, this archetype had to appear in a personal individual. If the archetype could not be realized in one personality, it could not be realized in the totality of individuals because the totality of deficient personalities together in no way represented the image of the ideal.[118]

Ullmann argued in a similar manner. According to him the idea of the human was a divine idea which would be empty and unessential if it were not realized. If among the thoughts of God as revealed to humankind, the idea of the human was the highest, then God could not have thought the idea of the human imperfectly, as caught up in eternal discord with human determination, but had to think the human perfectly. Because the idea was not a mere thought but something that bore in itself the guarantee of realization, the idea of the divine perfection of life had to become actual at some time in the course of human development; and since the perfection of life was not something abstract but concrete and individual, it had to be realized in a definite person. Because human determination consisted in a living community with God, i.e., in the union with God; because sin inwardly separated humankind from God, thereby effecting a split within the individual; because sin was a fact of experience that showed itself actually and prevented the person from attaining full consciousness of divine love, a personality like Christ was needed to cancel the contradiction existing in the human, to establish unity with God and the human, to effect reconciling redemption, and to found a religious community on its ground. With the recognition of sin, union with God could only be thought of as redemption and reconciliation. Both could only occur through an individual who stood outside of the realm of sin and in complete living community with God and who possessed the power to assume others into this communion. If the perfection of piety and morality was recognized as the highest human goal, if the highest goal of religion was the union of the human with God, and if one religion was the absolute religion, then this could be the case only if in the founder that unity was complete, i.e., if the founder was sinless. To consider Christianity absolute and its founder religiously or morally imperfect, Ullmann concluded, was inconsistent, a pure contradiction.[119]

Strauss and his critics affirmed the absoluteness of the Christian religion. By absoluteness both understood the perfection of the highest religious idea, the idea of the union of God and man. The point of difference between them was the way in which this idea was realized. Strauss's principle that the idea could only be realized in the endless course of time without history itself ever representing the idea perfectly was true only if the idea of God was resolved into the idea of humankind and vice versa. If the idea was God and God was the idea, if God had His reality and personality only in human life, then the human individual, as finite, could never be the adequate representation of infinite spirit or the infinite idea. World history could only be grasped as an endless process of life in which Absolute Spirit (the Idea) overcame the individual forms in order to return to itself in abstract infinity; the process would be continuously repeated.

The critics, on the other hand, conceived God as a personal God; the idea of humankind was seen as the eternal thought of God in which was grounded the divine creation of the human. And because the realization of the idea was conditioned by the absolute will of the personal God, the idea and its realization in one individual were co-determining. Thus, for the critics of Strauss, Strauss's speculative presupposition, if it was to be true, had to be completed: the idea was realized in humanity, but it was realized by and through individuals. All development in humankind, it was being asserted, rested on personalities, and all truly great personalities were significant in that their life was not isolated but went over into humankind and realized itself in it continuously. If the perfection of piety and morality was the highest goal of humankind and of each individual, then either it was realized in an individual personality or it was not realized at all, i.e., it was not an idea but fiction.

These assertions rested on two principles: 1) To assume that the idea of humanity was not at all realized was forbidden to modern criticism by the speculative standpoint itself which demanded that the idea not remain a mere ought but enter into reality. (For Strauss this reality was humankind.) 2) At the same time, speculative theology recognized the human as sinful and imperfect, and perfection could not result from imperfection. The moral-religious state, especially in its perfection, was one to which the concept of reciprocal completion did not apply: in the relationship to God, in a moral reference, each stood for her/himself and had a purely personal task and responsibility. Moral-religious perfection, consequently, was either totally present in one individual, or it was not there at all, i.e., it was not in the species. If the idea was fully realized in one individual, this did not mean that it was miserly toward all other individuals. In fact, the contrary was being asserted: only if the idea was realized in one individual, was that historical process introduced by virtue of which alone all other individuals could participate in the idea. It was seen as contradictory to assert something as belonging to the essence of humankind and to deny its realization in one individual; it was seen as incorrect and dangerous to consider divine nature immanent in human nature.

Thus, the rejection of Strauss's principle was essentially the affirmation of a personal God and of the value of the individual. Accordingly, a fundamental error responsible for Strauss's position concerning the realization of the idea was identified as pantheism. Conceding that the term pantheism tended to be used too casually, Schenkel found no more appropriate designation than that of pantheism for the abstract, dialectic view of God and the world that always aimed for the universal, for the idea. In the pantheism represented by Strauss, God was, to be sure, more than

Spinoza's substance; He was subject, life, and history, but He was not the Christian God.[120] As a consequence of his pantheistic tendency, Ullmann and Vorländer asserted, Strauss failed to recognize the significance of personality, of the individual in spiritual life. If it was true in other areas of life that ideas attained their effectiveness only to the extent that they found expression and externalization in individuals, consistency required that this be true also in spiritual life. In Christ, it was asserted, the idea of religion, God Himself, became personal to the extent that this was possible within human limitation.[121]

### d. Problem of Development

In maintaining that it was contrary to the laws of development to posit the initiator simultaneously as the greatest, Strauss, Kern asserted, overlooked two points. First, the appearance of Christ was already being prepared for in the Old Covenant by the introduction of the cancellation of the power and guilt of sin in humankind. Second, Christ was the founder of a total life, of a life that was, however, founded in connection with sin. If sin was to be cancelled and a new life begun, a new spiritual principle of life was needed which had to be present in the founder in a unique way. If this new principle were not so present, Kern concluded, the beginning of the new life would be incomprehensible.[122]

Strauss's presupposition, Schweizer stated, rested on misunderstanding and error, specifically on his inattention to the essence and nature of religion and of the founder of a religion. For Schweizer art, speculation, and religion were each a determination of self-consciousness. If analogies between the artistic and speculative areas and the religious area were found, the apparent contradictory nature of the claims of Christianity would be eliminated.

In both art and philosophy, Schweizer observed, the founder and master of a new principle retained his position of eminence and was not surpassed by his disciples. Admittedly, advancement and perfection of the initiated process occurred, but the fundamental view or insight remained unaffected by this, regarded always as the result of inspired vitality. Precisely this was being asserted by the Church. While theological demonstration and communication could advance, the life of faith in its intensive content, because perfect in its founder, was not subject to temporal perfectibility; faith was a matter of intuition and experience not of demonstration.

With respect to the founder of a religion, two conditions resulted from this. First, the inspired vitality of spirit, the source for all communities formed around one individual, lay in the region of spirit most immediately turned to the divine and offered an appropriate ground to account for the dignity of the founder of a religion. Secondly, the area of inspired self-consciousness, when referred to religion, was the only suitable ground in which revelation could take root: it was, in general, characteristic of genius not to be able to see her/his intuition as human but to be able to believe that she/he was impregnated by the divine.[123] The religious element in its very essence knew and felt itself to be absolutely dependent on God, to be an essentially unmediated act of God, i.e., to be revelation.[124]

According to Strauss it was also contradictory to the principles of development for a religious community to consider both itself and religious life in its totality to be perfect in its founder.[125] Speculative science offered no analogy for this assertion because in the area of knowledge what came earlier could be perfected by what came later. In art, however, perfection was not conditioned by time. Later generations did not necessarily surpass earlier ones, and the artistic achievements of one nation were not necessarily surpassed by the later masterpieces of another nation. This analogy, Schweizer admitted, did not totally parallel the religious area because the personal influence on those who were receptive was of a different kind.[126]

Schweizer's distinction between those areas of life in which one participated essentially by virtue of immediate self-consciousness and those in which one participated essentially by virtue of objective knowledge was based on Schleiermacher's epistemological principle according to which an inspired gift, an unmediated intuition, was essential to the former while the discursive faculty which was bound to mediation belonged to the latter. This difference accounted for the fact that each followed different laws and had a different course of development. If religion, like art and speculation, was a determination of self-consciousness, then its appearance and development could find analogies in areas proceeding from the determination of feeling. Although the analogies could not have escaped Strauss, his grasp of religion as something that was to be transformed into knowledge and the concept precluded recognition of them.

Strauss also asserted that any attempt to remove Jesus' God-consciousness or His human nature from the normal course of development was worthless since both were subject to conditions of finitude and imperfection. This raised the question as to whether it was externalities that determined individual personality and whether merely human nature remained if these were disregarded. Personality, it was asserted in terms reminiscent of Kant and Schleiermacher, was something internal, something rooted in the concept of human nature itself. Where it emerged forcefully, it was not conditioned and determined by externalities but drew the latter into itself as an organ of its effectiveness. While it was true that inner being was revealed in actions and that such actions were conditioned by time, place, and other individuals, it was not true that the uniqueness of the individual was thereby conditioned or constituted. Character as determined by free will was the individuality of the historical person. It was not this individuality, the free formation of spirit, that could be restricted but only its externally directed deed to the extent that it was externalized but not to the extent that it belonged to the free individual. The individuality of Christ, His historical appearance, was contained not in the temporal and natural but in His life and teaching. It was maintained that the essence of Christ could be concluded from the effect and the impression He made; from them arose, if history was approached without restrictive presuppositions, the intuition of a personality that included sinlessness as its most indispensable feature.[127]

Given the concept of religion and the concept of the human with which the critics of Strauss worked and acknowledging the idealistic and dogmatic framework in which they performed their demonstrations for the possibility and necessity of a sinless founder of the absolute religion, consistency and cogency cannot be denied their arguments. On the basis of their Christian idealism, Christianity was for them the absolute religion because what it taught concerning the highest idea of the human could not be surpassed. And because a religion arose through individuals, only that individual who embodied the idea of the morally-religiously perfect human being could be the founder of the absolute religion, i.e, the founder of the absolute religion had to be sinless.

Where the critics erred was in thinking that such speculative demonstration for the possibility (their concept of the human) and necessity (their concept of the absolute religion) of a sinless founder of the absolute religion guaranteed that history was recorded in the Gospels. For the critics speculative demonstrations provided the criteria for judging both the dogmatic and the historical truths of the teachings and claims of Christianity. Consequently, it was speculation that dictated the parameters within which historical criticism could rightfully operate. The task of historical criticism was to highlight those features and events in the image of the founder of Christianity as depicted by His contemporaries that could only be explained as the externalizations of a sinless essence. When the image presented by historical criticism approached the archetype of speculation, historical criticism attained the degree of certainty that could reasonably be expected of it: it showed how what was recorded of Christ fulfilled in particular the speculative and dogmatic requirements for the absolute religion and its sinless founder. The results of the investigation were established in advance of the investigation; only the details needed to be filled in. What the critics failed to hear was the implicit principle established by Strauss: the credibility of historical criticism was not dependent on speculative theology but rather the credibility of speculative theology, to the extent that any of its claims were conditioned by or pretended to condition history, had become dependent on historical criticism.

e. Miracles

A miracle is an event or act which because it cannot be comprehended from natural or historical connection is referred to divine effect and order, particularly when it is seen as coinciding with the purposes of revelation. Conceptually, miracles belong to every historical religion, and, thus, it was natural that miracles would be recorded in the history of Christianity as the revelation of God, i.e., that the life and activity of the Redeemer were accompanied by effects that bore the character of the miraculous. For Strauss historical consciousness and insight into the non-interruption of finite causation, i.e., into the impossibility of miracles, were inseparable concepts.[128] Consequently, he assumed the rejection of miracles as a legitimate principle of historical criticism. This rejection of miracles was also based on the similarity of events; difference was not excluded, but the difference could not obliterate all similarity.

It was objected that the so-called laws of causality were but the modes of perception for human self-consciousness; they were valid not in and of themselves but only until a higher mode of perception was found. As an example, the law of the impenetrability of bodies was offered, a law that prevailed until disproved by modern science.

Strauss was accused of inexcusable superficiality for appealing to the category of similarity, a category that was too indefinite to be a basic principle; from the known, it was argued, the essential content of the unknown could not be established in advance. Objection to this category was based on the conviction that because miracles belonged to a sphere that fell both within and outside of actual experience, they required a modification in the criteria that were applied to ascertain the correctness of knowledge concerning the world and the human.[129]

In response to Strauss's assertion in the third <u>Streitschrift</u> to the effect that the spiritual greatness and moral dignity of Jesus' speeches and conduct in His life and suffering were historical and that the first community added only the supernatural aspects, it was objected that such a separation was impossible since the narratives dealing with the miraculous contained a manifold of features belonging to the moral character of Jesus.[130]

While faith did not depend on any one particular miracle but rather on the manifestation of God's effectiveness in and through Christ whereby it was externally shown that God was with Him, the resurrection was an indispensable miracle. Without the resurrection neither Christ in His essence nor the founding of the Church would be thinkable. In the Christian view, the resurrection signified the victory of divine life over death and guaranteed that divine life was in Christ. No such guarantee was given if Christ were merely unconscious or apparently dead. While the mythic view recognized more of the religious significance of the resurrection than did this naturalistic or rationalistic view, it lacked, in the opinion of J. Müller, Kern, and Ullmann, convincing proof as to how belief in the resurrection originated. That the first Christian community would have created such an event for one who was supposed to be only a simple, popular teacher was not considered a plausible account for the resurrection.

Furthermore, even if the resurrection was a belief of current popular consciousness, the recorded expression of this consciousness in the Gospels did not in itself justify the conclusion that the resurrection was a myth. Disregarding the fact that such a procedure was in itself unscientific, the conclusion itself gave cause for suspicion since poetic interest played a subordinate role to the ethical concerns of the first Christian community. Two additional factors cast further suspicion on the correctness of the mythic view of the resurrection: 1) the type of miracle found in the Gospel was not the sensuous type of miracle generally connected with the Jewish conception of a Messiah according to which the Messiah was active in an earthly Kingdom of God and 2) the Apostles, who were supposed to have produced faith in the resurrection, were the ones who least expected it. Strauss, his critics concluded, wanted to direct interpretative attention away from the miraculous event itself to its narration in order to show how the narrative was able to originate without an historical foundation.[131]

The rejection of miracles was by no means unique to Strauss. Not only rationalists and naturalists but even avowed supernaturalists like Steudel attempted to rationalize the miracles, to remove from them those features that even the most literal of believers found difficult to accept. For Strauss, admittedly, the miraculous was in and of itself suspect. In addition, the attempts to harmonize conflicting reports and/or to minimize the extraordinary in order to make the recorded event more acceptable to the more sophisticated thought of the then modern age were often so contradictory and absurd that they in themselves would have been sufficient cause to drive a more critical thinker like Strauss to look for an explanation that made such exercises unnecessary. But it was not on these bases alone that Strauss rejected the miraculous. Rather, he looked at the documents not with the eyes of faith but with the eyes of an historical literary critic, and because he found evidence to support his theory that popular Messianic ideas rooted in the Old Testament were obviously present in the narratives, he concluded that these and not an historical fact were basic to the reports.

The critics looked at the narratives solely with the eyes of faith which is not to suggest that they accepted everything that was reported exactly as reported. They acknowledged that the work of criticism in the area of miracles could not be considered complete and that further investigation to determine the essential and unessential, the limits of tradition and of history were justified. They admitted that in and of itself the inexplicable moment had no religious or moral significance and that a miracle could only be properly interpreted when it was seen as part of Christ's redeeming activity and as part of the moral, religious, and spiritual power of Christ's personality and of the truth of His teachings--both of which were indispensable for the origination of the Church.

## 4. Concept of Myth and the Myth-Forming Process

In 1835, when Stauss published <u>Das Leben Jesu</u>, it was generally recognized that the Bible contained both symbolic and saga-like or mythic elements. The symbol and the saga or myth were the representations of a higher truth through a medium that was sensually more graspable than the idea that was being communicated. In the case of a symbol, this presentation was accomplished by means of a sign; in the case of myth, by means of words and actions. The symbol expressed the immediate and enduring relationship of the supersensuous to the world of the senses; the myth expressed that which was historically mediated. Consequently, what was conveyed in a myth externally appeared to be of a transitory nature; according to its inner meaning, however, the myth conveyed what was of lasting value. Because the myth availed itself of historical elements, it constituted a border area between idea and history, between the super- or pre-historical and the purely historical. While earlier mythic interpreters of the New Testament sought to distinguish mythic adornment from the true historical foundation, later mythic interpreters like de Wette and Usteri considered such a separation an impossibility because for them historical guise belonged to the essence of myth. Proponents of the mythic view did not consider the myth either deceptive or false but rather a necessary vehicle for religious ideas at a certain cultural level.

The sacraments as outward signs instituted by Christ to give grace were examples of the symbolic in the New Testament. While critics of Strauss were willing to admit of some mythic-like elements in the narratives preceding the public ministry of Jesus, they were convinced that the Gospels were fundamentally historical and not mythic: for the origin of the Christian Church could only be explained if the main content of the biblical tradition was historical, i.e., true; and the alleged absoluteness of Christianity required that it rest on historical grounds; otherwise, the idea of the God-man and the idea of the human remained a fiction. The arguments for the historical truth of the Gospels were offered in the intention of saving religious truth. However, these arguments did not proceed from historical investigations but from philosophical speculation on the necessity of the historical realization of the idea in one concrete individual. Philosophical, historical, and religious truth were so intertwined that legitimate conclusions in one area were transferred to another area without regard for the appropriateness or legitimacy of such a transfer.

An argument employed for the correctness of the historical view of the Gospels and against the mythic view was the argument of sufficient cause.[132] In essense, this was an argument against the idealizing tendency of the first community which, according to the mythic view, was responsible for the recorded image of Jesus. Ideas, it was asserted, could effect a good deal, but if they were to have a strong and lasting effect, they had to have a corresponding ground and occasion. Was it not more probable and far more in accordance with the analogy of historical development that a new community with a unique spirit and belief was formed by the creative effectivensss of a divinely endowed individual than that the ideal of such an individual was gradually formed by a community? The pivotal points in this argument were twofold: 1) the contradictions that the critics believed to have detected with respect to the role of the resurrection in Strauss's mythic view and 2) the effects that proceeded from and continually proceed from Christ.

As understood by the critics, the mythic view claimed that belief in Jesus' resurrection, itself the product of the Apostles' imagination, was so strong that it gave rise to belief in Him as the Messiah; from faith in the resurrection, everything else in His life was to be derived. While postulating that marvellous tales were already being told about Jesus during His lifetime, Strauss, it was asserted, left nothing in His life that would justify such aggrandizement. The mere relative excellence of Jesus could hardly be responsible for the fact that although He in no way corresponded to the then current Messianic expectation, His impression necessitated recognizing Him as the Messiah, but since the impression was not strong enough to sustain the recognition without fulfillment of the expectation, the imagination of the first Christians transferred to Jesus what He was lacking. This contradiction reflected a basic predisposition ascribed to Strauss by the critics. Strauss, it was asserted, tended to consider what was significant in the life of Jesus the product of invention, to see everything in His life as abstract and general, transformed into the concrete only by the saga. Strauss, it would appear, wanted to illustrate the principle that out of nothing, not only something, but something quite tremendous, a world-historical power, could arise.

With respect to the continuous and extraordinary efficaciousness of Christianity: the impression that Christ made on his contemporaries and continued to make on all successive generations, it was asserted, had to refer back with necessity to a unique individual, i.e., from the effects one had to conclude a cause that alone could account for the extraordinariness of the effects. This cause was posited as the consciousness of Christ: the nature of Christ's statements was such that they had to be considered the expression of a truly world-historical consciousness that reflected all of humankind as it related to the divine in itself and reflected itself in humankind. This world-historical consciousness in view of the indisputable effects attributed to it also had to be designated world-conquering and world-forming.[133]

It was the world-historical nature of Jesus' consciousness and the world-historical effects that proceeded from this consciousness that were to provide the norm for the conception of Jesus' personality: only the historical could be world-historical, and the world-historical according to its very essence could not be mythic. Revealed in Jesus was the realization of moral-religious perfection; the personal life externalized by Him was the life that then became through Him the life of humankind in general. Accordingly, moral receptivity was a requisite of any method that had the life of Jesus as its object. The appropriate procedure for historical criticism with respect to Christ was to produce and depict a living image of Christ in all its features and externalizations as harmonious and perfect in itself, i.e., to present Jesus in His holy, sinless essence and to present the effects of this image. For His contemporaries these effects were immediate; for all following generations they proceeded from the impression recorded by the Apostolic Age and preserved in the consciousness of the Church in the Apostolic writings and in the Christian community. Conviction as to the truth of the image, i.e., living inner certainty, arose, however, only when he to whom such an image was presented was open to and affected by it.

The contradiction that the critics emphasized with respect to the unaccountable idealization on the part of the first Christian community was rooted in their own philosophical and dogmatic presuppositions which prevented them from hearing what Strauss was saying. The critics themselves admitted that belief in the resurrection was the central belief for the Christian; the resurrection was, as it were, confirmation for the truth of Jesus' divinity, for the truth of His life. This was also being asserted by the mythic view, and to this extent the mythic view and the historical Christian view were in agreement. It is true that in the mythic view the resurrection was the product of the imagination. But the creation was not as arbitrary as the critics suggested, nor was the idealization as enigmatic as the critics were wont to conclude.

The second source stipulated by Strauss for the evangelical myth was the particular impression left by the personal character, actions, and fate of Jesus which served to modify the Messianic idea in the minds of His people. In accounting for the creation of the resurrection Strauss made two statements. He himself was probably unaware of their full significance. First, he stated that during the several years' intercourse with His disciples, Jesus had constantly impressed them more and more decidedly with the belief that He was the Messiah. Secondly, in accounting for the psychological necessity of the disciples to solve the contradiction between the fate of Jesus and their earlier opinion of Him, Strauss asserted that with the Jews of that age to comprehend meant nothing else than to derive from the Sacred Scriptures.[134] What Strauss was saying was that for those who first followed Christ He was the Messiah, and His impression was strong enough to effect modifications in the prevailing concept of the Messiah. This impression can be accounted for by appealing to the subjectivity, the dogmatic presuppositions, and the corresponding religious needs of those impressed. But this very appeal demands the shift in perspective that Strauss himself advocated but did not fully execute. Whether a concrete individual was necessary to initiate the process of the realization of the idea of the God-man and to ground the absoluteness of a religion was the concern of Strauss and his critics; it was not a constitutive element in the religious consciousness of the first Christian community. For the first Christians the man Jesus was not the idea of the Messiah, He was the promised Messiah. He was revelation the full significance of which could only be comprehended by searching Scripture in order to explain revelation within revelation.[135]

Because Strauss identified the myth with the unhistorical, he pronounced the Bible an unhistorical document, and because it was unhistorical, Strauss, despite, or perhaps because of, his insight into the totally religious nature of the biblical myth, concluded that because it was without historical truth, there was nothing more that could be done with the Bible, for whatever religious truth it contained would be more perfectly expressed and known as philosophical truth. The contradiction detected in Strauss, consequently, lies not so much in the fact that the Jesus of history as depicted by him could scarcely account for the biblical Christ but rather in the fact that an intuited historical phenomenon in human religious history, that which Strauss termed the myth-forming process, was undervalued in its historical significance. And it was undervalued not on the basis of a principle of historical criticism but on the basis of a philosophical principle: the religious representation had to be negated so that the religious content might be raised to the concept.

The intended historical argument from effect to cause developed by the critics rested solely on philosophical and doctrinal presuppositions: the posited historical fact was the subjectivity of Christ the religious and moral perfection of which was to be concluded from the morally and religiously liberating effects associated with the new life initiated by Him. An attempt to reconstruct historically the historical, religious, and doctrinal milieu in which the Gospels were formed was not advocated; proposed was a psychological analysis to determine the inner life of Jesus. The Gospels were to be used as historical documents that yielded biographical material, a purpose for which they were little suited. This psychological approach proceeded from the assumption that the statements of Christ and the main events in His life were historically accurate, that they were the written documentation of the realization of the idea of the God-man and of the sinless founder of the absolute religion. Were this approach followed consistently, Christianity would become a completely subjective phenomenon.

For both the mythic view of Strauss and the psychological approach of the critics, Christianity was the realization of an idea: for the former Christianity was the historical form assumed by the idea at a necessary stage in its development; for the latter the subjectivity of Christ was the historical form of this same idea. In the former view Christianity actually had a surer foundation in history than in the latter view, for in it the potential existed for considering the historical and religious truth of Christianity within the historical framework of biblical tradition whereas in the psychological view the emphasis on subjectivity both with respect to cause and effect reduced an historical religious phenomenon to the proclamation of an idea.

When critics turned their attention directly to Strauss's definition of myth and his own account of the myth-forming process responsible for the New Testament narratives, they detected a contradiction between the definition of myth to which scientific accuracy was ascribed and the criteria Strauss himself proposed for determining the presence of myth.

Myth was defined as an unconscious self-objectification of the idea in a fact posited by the creative production of the idea. This definition of myth suggested three tasks for the mythic interpreter: 1) to indicate the fundamental ideas embodied in the myth; 2) to demonstrate the necessity of these ideas; and 3) to show how the narratives were the unconscious expression of these ideas objectifying themselves.[136]

It was objected that while it was fundamental to Strauss's mythic treatment of the Gospels that in the earliest communities the true consciousness of the unity of the divine and human was present, albeit in an inadequate form, only in the conclusion of his work where no determinations were possible did he introduce this idea. In the historical section, where particulars were treated, Strauss gave no indication as to how it happened that the unconscious poetry of the earliest communities expressed this idea precisely in the mythic form. According to Strauss's explanation, the biblical narrative generally was not formed from an idea but from the thread of external references and analogies, often through the mediation of the most arbitrary and insignificant occasion. Nor was the necessity of the entrance of the idea into spiritual life demonstrated in such a way that the myth was shown to be the expression of this level of development resulting of itself, i.e., it was not shown how exactly at that time the idea necessarily dawned on humankind without an individual personality corresponding to it. With respect to the third task, myth had to be unconscious in its attempt to give expression to higher truth; once it was aware through historical sense or philosophy of its own significance, it was no longer myth. For myth to arise the idea could only be known in the reflection of its image; it could not yet be the object of thought. But in the Bible ideas were being communicated directly through teaching, i.e., abstract thought existed, and the presence of the parables spoke for a more developed intellectual level than myth formation would permit. Thus, conditions requisite to unconscious myth formation were neither present when Jesus lived nor did Strauss find them present. Rather, Strauss treated all four Gospels as conscious productions; intentionality (the purpose of glorifying a definite historical individual) and reflection (the transfer of already existing features and views to a given object) preceded them all.[137]

The contradiction found between Strauss's definition of myth and his account of the origin of the biblical myths was also behind Geier's criticism of Strauss and Weisse's attempt to find analogies for so-called myths that arose around individuals whose historical existence was unquestionable.

Geier undertook a comparison of the myths told of Alexander the Great (his conception and birth, childhood stories, events from later life) and the so-called biblical myths and concluded that according to the criteria established by Strauss, the narratives told about Alexander the Great would have to be called myths. But while these narratives could be designated unhistorical embellishments, fables, fairytales, or anecdotes, they were not myths in the strict sense of the term. While Strauss usually designated these narratives myths, he also referred to them as anecdotes or sagas, from which followed, Geier concluded, that Strauss himself confused myth, anecdote, and unhistorical saga.[138]

According to Weisse the life of every significant historical personality, be he poet, philosopher, artist, statesman, or hero, was embellished by myths. These personalities lived within a totally historical age and were known according to their historically significant deeds and fates. Nonetheless, they became the objects of mythic tales not in some distant time but by the following generation, if not already by their own contemporaries. Two features distinguished these myths: 1) their conformity to the spirit of history and to the completely individual, personal character and 2) their sensitive, figurative expression of this spirit. To the extent that myths might be present in the biblical narratives, this kind of myth was to provide an analogy: with it Christ remained a completely known historical personality comparable to, though hardly the same as, Alexander the Great. That such myths which did not invent Christ's divine dignity nor His Messianic calling could arise within the circle of His disciples, Weisse concluded, could only be denied by those who permitted no scientific criticism of the Gospels.[139]

Because myth was a tradition that proceeded from the idea and clothed the idea in the form of history and saga was a tradition that proceeded from history and reflected the historical in the realm of the ideal, Weisse's suggested analogy actually fell more within the domain of saga than within that of pure myth. In general, the critics were less uncomfortable when the term saga was used to designate those parts of the Gospel, e.g., the childhood narratives, that incorporated mythic-like elements. The term saga was preferred because as a concept it was not incompatible with the fundamental conviction that the essential content of what was being transmitted was a fact, something that actually occurred and concerned or proceeded from an historical person.

While Strauss distinguished between myth and saga, he made no use of the distinction in his presentation. What suggests itself as a credible explanation for Strauss's selection of the term myth as the most appropriate designation for the process he was describing is the connection he made between representation and myth. Myth was <u>the</u> subject of investigation at that time; it had already been established and accepted by many biblical exegetes as a concept that permitted the Bible to regain its dignity as a religious, if not an historical, document. Since the Bible contained religious representations, the term myth, in all likelihood, struck Strauss as the term that best served his scientific purpose without involving the biblical authors in deception or fraud.

In view of the definition of myth that was accepted by both Strauss and his critics, the critics were correct in accusing Strauss of being unfaithful to this definition, for the criteria he established for what he envisioned as the myth-forming process were incompatible with this definition. As described by Strauss the origin of the biblical myth was not the <u>unconscious</u> creative activity that was recognized as the essential component of myth; what Strauss termed the biblical myth did seem to lack the inherent vitality that was being emphasized by the critics. Implicit in Strauss's presentation of the origin of the biblical narratives was the external, provable purpose of glorifying a definite historical individual; transferred to Jesus were modifications of already existing features and views. To this extent, biblical poetry would have to be pronounced void of an indwelling productive force. In terms of the more positive concept of myth, the New Testament narratives, to the extent that anything mythic could be found in them, were, at best, dead afterbirths of genuinely poetic myths.

The critics, however, were wrong in inferring from this that the process described by Strauss, since it could not be called mythic, degraded the Gospel to an invented work of deceptive intentionality. There is nothing in Strauss's criteria or in his explication of these criteria that warrants such an inference; on the contrary, Strauss was anxious to emphasize that the biblical authors could not be accused of any intentional deception or pious fraud. And contrary to the view of the critics, Strauss did indicate the idea behind the biblical myth: the idea of the Messiah. His entire critical section aims at showing how this idea found expression in the subjective representations of the first Christian community, from which the apparent facts, as the historical guise of these representations, were supposed to have been formed. The idea of the God-man was, as it were, latent in the representations formed around and from the idea of the Messiah.

While the critics were content to show the scientific unsuitability of the term myth and were convinced that by highlighting the contradiction between the definition and the criteria, they had established the inapplicability of both to the Gospels, their refutation applied only to the term myth itself but not to the process. The critics looked at the process not in itself but only in its relationship to the concept of myth. Because the process could not be called mythic, it did not follow that it in no way captured something of the historical, spiritual, reflective process that resulted in the Gospels. Although the critics correctly identified the two elements of this process that were fundamental to Strauss's position, vis., the glorification of the historical Jesus and the transference of already existing views and ideas to Him, they misunderstood the function of these elements.

The glorification and the transference were not, nor did Strauss understand them to be, of the prosaic nature suggested by the critics. The glorification was not the inexplicable bestowal of extraordinary honor and fame on a simple Jewish teacher; rather, it was the identification of those religious and moral qualities experienced in Christ that explained His appearance as that of One particularly favored by God. The glorification implied by Strauss was not intended to convey the self-worship of the human but the exaltation of God Who was revealing Himself in the person Jesus. Jesus was experienced as the Promised Messiah; hence the transference of those qualities from the Old Testament prophecies that seemed to explain the new revelation. The glorification occurred by means of the transference; this religious act of transference was itself the expression of the spiritual experience of transcendent Being.

For the religious Jew history was not merely secular; history was sacred history. Significant events that occurred were meditated upon in an attempt to understand the action of God in them. The source for such understanding was Scripture. The religious past was never forgotten; the present was understood in terms of this past, and when adapted to new changed circumstances, the past served as a guide or program for the future. In searching Scripture biblical interpreters did not simply reproduce what was already written. Scripture contained the Word of God; it was a living tradition, and the biblical authors responded to this living tradition by further developing and enriching what was contained in it.

When investigations into the nature of myth were first undertaken, it was thought possible that the historical fact basic to the historical myth could be uncovered. But since only subjective criteria for such a separation were offered, it became apparent that for the sake of scientific credibility, such separation was an impossibility. While this inseparability of the historical and its mythic adornment was initially not a denial of the historical, it was this feature that permitted the identification of the mythic with the unhistorical. And it was at this point that the myth became capable of accommodating a religious presupposition: if one were convinced that human history excluded the possibility of the supernatural, then the supernatural as the unhistorical could be termed mythic. The myth was no longer just the designation for a literary genre; rather, it had become the expression for a religious judgment.

While Strauss's theory correctly emphasized the subjective reflections involved in the biblical narratives, his identification of the resulting representations with the mythic mode of thought precluded further investigation both with respect to differences and similarities between the Bible and other ancient religious writings and with respect to the religious tradition and the religious thought matrix of the biblical authors. While their mode of thought may have been sensual, certainly it did not indicate a poverty in concept and word nor such an unfamiliarity with natural causality that would in itself explain the nature of the interruption in the natural course of events that was recorded in the Gospel. In the final analysis Strauss's historical sense promised more than it delivered. Strauss put the New Testament within the biblical tradition and sought to explain the historical genesis of the Bible within its historical, religious, and doctrinal milieu. However, despite Strauss's claims to the contrary, his historical-critical investigation of the Gospels was influenced by his understanding of the speculative principle concerning the relationship between representation and concept, his identification of representation, the primitive stage of the enlightened concept, with myth, and the implied identification of the mythical with the unhistorical, i.e., with the untrue. And while Strauss's interest was supposedly with the historical myth, his concept of historical myth verged on the philosophical, for as Strauss develops his explication of the myth-forming process, what frequently seems implied is that the biblical authors interwove history into their own ideas of the Messiah (with Jesus as the source for the modifications of the Old Testament conceptions) and/or that the historical element consisted in the reflection of the spirit of the people. These implications which are contrary to Strauss's assertion that historical events were fundamental to most biblical narratives attest to the elusive nature of any attempt to specify finely the conditions under which and by means of which a myth arises.

Although the critics falsely accused Strauss of undertaking a critical investigation of the Gospels, the results of which were already predetermined by the speculative presuppositions revealed in his Christology, they were correct in maintaining that the historical-critical section was not presuppositionless. At the same time they could not suspend their own philosophical and theological presuppositions to give a fair evaluation of the historical methodology suggested by Strauss for the origin of the biblical narratives. The absoluteness of Christianity which was supported by speculative demonstrations and dogmatic presuppositions determined for the critics the direction that was to be taken by historical criticism. With respect to historical criticism of the Gospels, no dialogue was possible between Strauss and his critics because for Strauss, at least according to his intention, the biblical Christ was conditioned by what could be determined about the historical Jesus, whereas for the critics, the historical Jesus was conditioned by what was believed about the biblical Christ as the sinless founder of the absolute religion.

Chapter Four

Conclusion

The relationship between historical facts and faith was a central concern to the critics considered here. But these critics showed little understanding for the historical-critical method, for that investigation of written documents that seeks to determine their character and reliability as historical reports. Rather the critics proceeded either from dogmatic or from philosophical principles, and it was these principles that conditioned their pronouncements about the historical veracity of the biblical narratives. According to those who argued from the former standpoint, the Bible was history; in it was contained the written record of the life, suffering, and death of the man Jesus Who was the incarnate God. While some concessions might be granted, these concessions essentially left the written record in tact as an historical document. But the history so recorded was history only for the believer, only for the one who believed that Jesus was the Lord and Founder of the absolute religion.

For those who argued more from philosophical presuppositions, it was the realization of the idea, be it the idea of the God-man or that of the absolute religion, that vouchsafed the historical nature of the Gospel narratives. These idealistically influenced defenders of the Bible viewed the biblical narratives as the documentation of the concrete historical realization of an idea which were it not so realized would remain empty. Since this idea had to be realized in time and since what was reported of the man Jesus so perfectly fleshed out the idea of the sinless founder of the absolute religion, it followed necessarily that the Gospels were historical.

Correctly emphasized by means of the dogmatic assumptions was the religious and moral significance of the Gospels. But the unsurpassed excellence of their religious and moral content became the guarantee for the historical truth of the Gospels; anything fictitious, contrived, or invented was automatically precluded. In addition, proponents of this position correctly perceived that the Gospels were primarily religious history, that the historical material basic to them was presented not for itself but to satisfy specifically religious needs, and that the biblical authors were not primarily historians but men filled with religious enthusiasm who wanted to bring others to an awareness of salvation through Jesus Christ. But these insights stopped there. Dogmatic belief prevented these theologians from seeing the biblical narratives as anything but eyewitness accounts of events that had actually occurred as reported. And while the intent of these defenders was certainly the restoration of lost dignity to the Bible, they failed in their attempt to do this. For although they pronounced the Bible an historical document, it was not to be treated as such. These very theologians wanted to raise the Gospels above history in the conviction that the normal standards for judging historical truth could not be applied to a content that was primarily religious or moral, and/or they wanted historical criticism to be satisfied with highlighting those features in the life of Jesus that corresponded to the moral and religious spirit that generally was not denied to the Gospels. Thus, the inchoate intuition that the Bible may not contain eyewitness accounts but rather a living testimony of faith written to inspire and sustain faith in a living religious community was dropped and an inconsistent position continued to be maintained.

For those who argued from speculative presuppositions, historical criticism was merely an exercise in confirmation; its task was to specify in particular the way in which certain ideas were realized. According to proponents of this position, the truth of what was recorded in the Gospels was established once it had been shown that the fundamental teachings of Christianity agreed with certain ideas, the truth and necessity of which had been demonstrated philosophically. The idea of man and the idea of the God-man had to be realized if they and the absoluteness of Christianity that was directly related to them were not to remain empty concepts. Since the concept of religion from which these speculative theologians proceeded ascribed a significant role to the individual, the ideas had to be realized only in and by an individual. And since the absoluteness of a religion necessitated a founder who was morally and religiously perfect, i.e., sinless, it followed that Jesus was who and what He said He was. An historical judgment was, thus, the direct conclusion of philosophical principles.

Proponents of this position were cavalier in their attitude toward historical criticism. In the conviction that historical criticism lacked an inherent standard whereby its results could be pronounced with any degree of certainty, they pointed it in the direction that would permit it to reach the degree of certainty that could reasonably be expected of it.

What separated the critics who argued from dogmatic presuppositions from those who argued from speculative presuppositions was that for the former religious truth was at issue, whereas the absoluteness of Christianity constituted the primary concern of the latter. The absoluteness of Christianity need not necessarily exclude an interest in religious truth, but what emerged in the arguments of the critics was not so much concern for religious truth as concern that the idea of the God-man--which was the original, divine idea of humankind--not remain an empty concept. The disposition to religious perfection was, in this view, inherent in the concept of the human; a human being, therefore, would never be able to realize this religious potential unless Christ was the sinless man.

Be it on dogmatic or on speculative grounds, for the critical consciousness that revealed itself in the criticism exercised on Strauss, Jesus was what He said He was. When attention was turned specifically to Strauss's account of the origin of the biblical narratives, criticism found it impossible to maintain this belief and simultaneously to consider an account of the way in which a like belief may have come to assume the particular form it took in the biblical narratives. In trying to dismiss Strauss's theory either by showing the incorrectness of his philosophical position or the contradiction between the concept of myth and Strauss's application of this concept, critical consciousness simply avoided the historical questions. The argument from sufficient cause which was to be the argument against the suggested idealizing tendency of the first community was actually an example of that which it was intended to refute. For with it extraordinary effects were being attributed not, as in the case of the first Christian community, to an extraordinary man but to the extraordinary consciousness that accounted for the extraordinary man. Critical consciousness, thus, moved the discussion from the area of the historical to that of the psychological. Behind the move was belief in the redeemed state of humankind. For some this belief remained purely a matter of religious conviction; for others the religious belief was strengthened by virtue of the fact that what the Church taught concerning redemption agreed with the results of speculative theology.

Thus, the charge leveled by the critics against Strauss is applicable to critical consciousness in general. Preoccupied

with its own perspective, it neglected to pay fair attention to
the historical method proposed by Strauss and simply proceeded to
justify its own presuppositions and to make historical criticism
the handmaiden of these principles.

Abbreviations used in the footnotes and the bibliography.

1. Works by Strauss
AB: Ausgewählte Briefe von David Friedrich Strauss
 "An meine Mutter:" Zum Andenken an meine gute Mutter
GS: Gesammelte Schriften
LD: Literarische Denkwürdigkeiten
LJ: The Life of Jesus Critically Examined
S: Streitschriften zur Vertheidigung meiner Schrift über das Leben Jesu

2. Journals
J f a th Lit.: Journal für auserlesene theologische Literatur
Krit. Journal: Kritisches Journal der neuesten theologischen Literatur
TSuK: Theologische Studien und Kritiken
TZ: Tübinger Zeitschrift für Theologie
Z für h Th: Zeitschrift für historische Theologie
Z für Ph: Zeitschrift für Philosophie und spekulative Theologie

## NOTES

[1] Kern, "Erörterung der Hauptthatsachen der evangelischen Geschichte, in Rücksicht auf Strauss's Schrift: 'Das Leben Jesu,'" TZ, 1836, No. 2, p. 14.

[2] Ullmann, "Das Leben Jesu," TSuK, 1836, IX, No. 3, p. 772.

[3] AB, 10 April 1841, to Rapp.

[4] The biographical material that follows is based on Strauss's memorial to his mother, "An meine Mutter," GS 1, pp. 81-104.

[5] "Christian Märklin," GS 10, "Justinus Kerner," GS 1. The material that follows is based on these sources.

[6] "Justinus Kerner," GS 1, p. 125.

[7] ibid., p. 128.

[8] Zeller, David Friedrich Strauss, p. 21.

[9] "Christian Märklin," p. 223. ("doppelten Antrieb, da weiter vorzudringen, wo der Meister, ziemlich willkürlich, wie es uns vorkommen wollte, Gränzphäle gesteckt hatte, der ewige Friede, den er zwischen Philosophie und Theologie abgeschlossen zu haben sich rühmte, erschien uns nur als ein gebrechlicher Waffenstillstand, und wir fanden gerathen, uns auf den Kriegsfall vorzusehen.")

[10] ibid.

[11] ibid. ("Während der Verstand in die schärfste dialektische Schule genommen wurde, boten sich dem Geiste die tiefsten Ahnungen, der Phantasie die überraschendsten Ausblicke; die ganze Weltgeschichte zog in neuer Beleuchtung an uns vorüber; Kunst und Religion in ihren verschiedenen Formen tauchten an ihrer Stelle auf, und dieser ganze Reichtum an Gestalten ging aus dem Einen Selbstbewusstsein hervor und wieder und wieder in dasselbe zurück, das sich damit als die Macht aller Dinge kennen lernte.")

[12] AB, 12/22 November 1830, to Märklin.

[13] AB, 26 Dezember 1830, to Märklin.

14_AB_, 31 Mai 1831, to Märklin. v. also "Christian Märklin," p. 240, where Strauss states that he, Märklin, and other friends had plans to go to Berlin to hear the revered masters Hegel and Schleiermacher.

15These occurred at a time when Switzerland was undergoing reforms. Strauss's appointment was linked with the radical movement and incited the conservative opposition. Cf. Hausrath, David Friedrich Strauss 1, pp. 351f.; Ziegler, David Friedrich Strauss 1, pp. 288-394; Anon., "Der Kampf der Principien in Canton Zürich im Jahre 1839," Z f h Th, 1830, X, No. 3, pp. 94-116.

16_AB_, 24 Februar 1849, to Vischer. ("kunstlerischer Wissenschaftler)

17_AB_, 5 April 1831, to Rapp.

18_LD_, pp. 8-10.

19_AB_, 3 Juni 1846, to Vischer.

20_LD_, pp. 11-12.

21ibid., p. 30. ("er musste dem Licht, der Freiheit zugekehrt, musste ein Feind der Despoten und der Pfaffen sein.")

22ibid., p. 4.

23_AB_, 18 Juli 1863, to Vischer.

24_LD_, p. 7.

25_AB_, 13 Oktober 1850, to Vischer. ("Zur Philosophie als solcher habe ich kein Talent.")

26_AB_, 22 Juli 1846, to Märklin.

27_AB_, 1 Oktober 1843, to Wilhelm Strauss.

28Harris, David Friedrich Strauss, pp. ix-x.

29Müller, Identität und Immanenz, p. 262. ("jenes tiefere sachliche Verständnis für die Eigen-Art des Theologischen und Religiösen.")

30_AB_, 24 September 1862, to Gervinus. ("Ich komme von der Anklage des Schicksals zuletzt immer wieder auf die Selbstanklage zurück, dass ich beharrlicher, weniger empfindlich hätte sein und aus dem Faden, den ich einmal fest gefasst hätte, fortspinnen sollen.")

[31] Hartlich and Sachs, *Der Ursprung des Mythosbegriffes*, p. 3.

[32] ibid., p. 3.

[33] v. on the Mythic School, Hartlich and Sachs, *Der Ursprung des Mythosbegriffes*, pp. 11f, and Harris, *David Friedrich Strauss*, pp. 259f.

[34] Hartlich and Sachs, *Der Ursprung des Mythosbegriffs*, p. 14.

[35] ibid., p. 13.

[36] ibid., p. 18.

[37] ibid., p. 20.

[38] ibid., p. 24.

[39] ibid., pp. 31-32.

[40] ibid., p.22.

[41] ibid.

[42] ibid., pp. 32-33.

[43] *LJ*, p. 66.

[44] Gabler, "Ist es erlaubt in der Bibel und sogar im Neuen Testamente Mythen anzunehmen?" *J f a th L*, 11, No. 1, p. 43. The discussion that follows is based on this article, pp. 43-53.

[45] Hartlich and Sachs, *Der Ursprung des Mythosbegriffs*, pp. 69-85.

[46] ibid., pp. 91-96.

[47] ibid., p. 102, ("den ersten Stand der Diskussion um das Verhältnis von Mythos and Historie, wie es mit der Einführung des Mythosbegriffes in die Bibelwissenschaft zum unvermeidlichen Problem werden musste-und zwar gerade auf dem Boden einer gemeinsamen Grundanschauung, für welche das *Vorliegen* von mythischen Bestandteilen in der Bibel selbst keine Frage mehr darstellte.") Emphasis in original.

[48] ibid., pp. 111-119.

[49] Müller, *Identität und Immanenz*, p. 192.

[50] Harris, David Friedrich Strauss, pp. 270f.

[51] Sandberger, David Friedrich Strauss, p. 151.

[52] Harris, David Friedrich Strauss, p. 265.

[53] ibid., pp. 265f.

[54] ibid., pp. 266-67.

[55] ibid., p. 268.

[56] "Ueber die verschiedenen Rücksichten, in welchen und für welche der Biograph Jesu arbeiten kann," Krit. Journal., V, No. 3, pp. 230-43. This article is translated in full in the appendix.

[57] ibid., pp. 243-45.

[58] Harris, David Friedrich Strauss, pp. 269-70.

[59] Usteri, "Beytrag zur Erklärung der Versuchungsgeschichte," TSuK, 1832, V. No. 4, pp. 768-91.

[60] Sandberger, David Friedrich Strauss, p. 148.

[61] ibid., pp. 148f.

[62] Cromwell, David Friedrich Strauss, pp. 42-45.

[63] LD, p. 4. ("inspirirtes Buch; d.h. der Verfasser hatte den mächtigsten Entwicklungstrieb der damaligen theologischen Wissenschaft in sich aufgenommen, und aus diesem Trieb ging das Buch hervor.") In this work, Strauss also acknowledged that the concessions made in the third edition of Das Leben Jesu were not a true reflection of his position. He attributed the concessions to the fact that the mood out of which the book had originally been written was no longer present, pp. 5-6. These concessions included granting Jesus a more significant role in Christianity without, however, diminishing the role of myth, questioning the inauthenticity of John, and admitting that some of the miracles performed by Jesus might be true. This last concession was based on assumed psycho-emotional powers of Jesus and on magnetism. The concessions were made when Strauss was at a low ebb emotionally and when the possibility for a professorship at Zürich was still open.

⁶⁴AB, 6 February 1832, to Märklin. ("[I]ch bin oft recht traurig, dass Alles, was ich in der Theologie thun möchte, nur solche halsbrechende Arbeit ist. Aber ich kann es nicht ändern; auf irgend eine Weise muss dieser Stoff aus mir herausgestaltet werden . . . Und ich will vorher lesen und dann erst schreiben. Wir wollen es einstweilen Gott befehlen, der uns doch irgendwie eine Thür für so etwas öffnen wird.")

⁶⁵S, Heft 111, pp. 57f. The discussion that follows is based on these two sources and on Das Leben Jesu.

⁶⁶LJ, §13, §15.

⁶⁷AB, 6 Februar 1832, to Märklin. ("Auf diese Weise würde ich [Strauss] den unendlichen Inhalt, welchen der Glaube an diesem Leben hat, theils vernichten, theils wankend machen- freilich nur um ihn in höherer Weise wieder herzustellen.")

⁶⁸S, Heft 111, p. 59.

⁶⁹LJ, §151.

⁷⁰Strauss develops his concept of myth and his criteria for the pure evangelical myth in Das Leben Jesu, sections 8-16.

⁷¹LJ, §15.

⁷²ibid, §16.

⁷³ibid.

⁷⁴ibid., §151.

⁷⁵cf. Edgar Quinet, "Ueber das Leben Jesu, von Dr. Strauss," Excerpts. O. Schwab, trans. From the Revue des deux Mondes, Dec. 1838, TZ, 1839, No. 4, pp. 2-22; Kern, "Erörterung der Hauptthatsachen der evangelischen Geschichte, in Rücksicht auf Strauss's Schrift: 'Das Leben Jesu'," TZ, 1836, No. 2, p. 16; 1838, No. 2, p. 7; Ullmann, "Das Leben Jesu," TSuK, 1836, IX, No. 3, pp. 776-80; Julius Müller, "Das Leben Jesu," TSuK, 1836, IX, No. 3, pp. 816-18; p. 884.

⁷⁶LJ, §151.

[77] Kern, "Erörterung der Hauptthatsachen," _TZ_, 1836, No. 2, pp. 50-51. ("Eine unpartheiische Kritik wird nie blos negativ sich verhaltend auf die Versuchung des vermutheten Unwahren ausgehen, sondern sie wird sich zugleich auch positiv verhalten, und das Wesentliche der Wahrheit zu ermitteln bemüht seyn. Die Strauss' sche Kritik aber hat vorzugsweise nur eine negative Seite, und ihre positive Seite ist lediglich nur auf den Zweck hingerichtet, das durch die negative Kritik in sich Aufgelöste, als eine Fiktion nachzuweisen, als eine Fiktion bald der mehr unabsichtlich wirkenden Sage, bald aber auch der absichtlichen Dichtung.") Emphasis in original. cf. also Friedrich Vörlander, "Ueber die philosophisch-theologische Theorie des Dr. Strauss, Verfasser des Lebens Jesu," _Z für Ph_, lll, No. 1, pp. 77-78; Ullmann, "Das Leben Jesu," _TSuK_, 1836, IX, No. 3, p. 775; p.783.

[78] _LJ_, pp. 757-58.

[79] Steudel, "Vorläufig zu Beherzigendes," _TZ_, 1835, No. 3, pp. 194-96. cf. August Hahn, "Für grammatisch-historische Interpretation und gegen traditionelle, philosophische und allegorische. Ein vorläufiger Versuch," _TSuK_, 1830, lll, No. 2, pp. 312-13; Ullman, "Das Leben Jesu," _TSuK_, 1836, IX, No. 3, p. 775.

[80] Steudel, "Vorläufig zu Beherzigendes," _TZ_, 1835, No. 3, pp. 194-96.

[81] Stäudlin, "Ueber die blos historische Auslegung der Bücher der Neuen Testaments," _Krit. Journal_, 1, No. 4, pp. 337-39, II, No. 1, p. 5.

[82] ibid., I. No. 4, p. 337.

[83] ibid., II, No. 1, pp. 11-32; II, No. 2, pp. 126-28.

[84] Gelpke, "Ueber den richtigen Standpunkt einer Kritik der evangelischen Geschichte," _Z für Ph_, IV, No. 2, pp. 255-59.

[85] ibid., p. 265.

[86] ibid., pp. 265-66.

[87] Beck, "Ueber mythische Auffassung der neutestamentlichen Evangelien-Urkunden, ein Beitrag zu deren theologischen Würdigung." _TZ_, 1835, No. 4, p. 65.

[88] ibid., p. 67 ("das Christenthum lässt es einmal nicht sich nehmen, dass sein Paraklet nur mit der strengsten Wahrheit zusammen sey, und unter seinem Siegel kein menschliches Gedichte könne auftreten.")

⁸⁹Ullman, "Das Leben Jesu," <u>TSuK</u>, 1836 IX, No. 3, pp. 800-01.

⁹⁰ibid., p. 803.

⁹¹ibid., p. 804.

⁹²ibid., pp. 804-06.

⁹³<u>S</u>, Heft 111, p. 37. ("Man kann es mit einem Worte aussprechen, was die Voraussetzung der historischen Kritik ausmacht: es ist die wesentliche Gleichartigkeit alles Geschehen.")

⁹⁴<u>LJ</u>, p. lii.

⁹⁵ibid.

⁹⁶<u>S</u>, Heft 1, pp. 92-93. ("In wissenschaftlichen Dingen verhält der Geist sich frei: soll also auch freimüthig das Haupt erheben, nicht knechtisch es senken; für die Wissenschaft existirt unmittelbar kein Heiliges, sondern nur Wahres: dieses aber verlangt keine Weihrauchwolken der Andacht, sondern Klarheit des Denkens und Redens; noch kennt der Geist, wo er der Spur der Wahrheit zu folgen sich bewusst ist, eine Gefahr: sondern ist völlig ruhig über das Ziel, zu welchem sie ihn führen wird, überzeugt, es werde das besste sein. Alles jenes andächtige, beklemmte Wesen aber in Sachen der Wissenschaft kann nur dazu dienen, das Denken scheu und befangen zu machen, es durch fremdartige Rücksichten zu bestechen, und statt zum Ziele der Wahrheit vorwarts, vielmehr in Kreise dahin zurückzuführen, wo das Vorurtheil längst stand, und auch fernerhin zu verbleiben wünscht.")

⁹⁷Ullmann, "Das Leben Jesu," <u>TSuK</u>, 1836, IX, No. 3, p. 778.

⁹⁸Schweizer, "Das Leben Jesu von Strauss im Verhältnisse zur Schleiermacher'schen Dignität des Religionsstifters," <u>TSuK</u>, 1837, X, No. 3, p. 461.

⁹⁹Schenkel "Ueber die neuesten Bearbeitung des Lebens Jesu," <u>TSuK</u>, 1840, XIII, No. 3, p. 742.

¹⁰⁰Vorländer, "Ueber die philosophische-theologische Theorie des Dr. Strauss, Verfasser des Lebens Jesu," <u>Z für Ph</u>, 111, No. 1, pp. 70-71, ("mit klaren Bewusstseyn . . . mit rücksichtsloser wissenschaftlicher Consequenz . . . Was in der Religionsphilosophie Hegels bald ausgesprochen, bald versteckt wird: das Christus als der erlösende Sohn Gottes Produkt der Gemeinde, der Kirche sei,

nicht aber wirkliche göttliche Thatsache . . . dies ist es, was Strauss unumwunden lehrt und in seiner Kritik durchzuführen sucht.")

[101] Müller, "Das Leben Jesu," TSuK, 1836, IX, No. 3, p. 838, ("das Produkt eines gewissen Fanatismus der Spekulation")

[102] ibid.

[103] S, Heft 111, p. 57. ("Mit der Hegel' schen Philosophie stand meine Kritik des Lebens Jesu von ihrem Ursprung an in innerem Verhältniss.")

[104] ibid. ("ob der historische Charakter zum Inhalt mitgehöre, welcher, für Vorstellung und Begriff derselbe, auch von dem letztern Anerkennung fordere; oder ob er zur blosen Form zu schlagen, mithin das begreifende Denken an ihn nicht gebunden sei.")

[105] cf. Ullman, "Polemisches in Betreff der Sündlosigkeit Jesu, mit besonderer Rücksicht auf D. Chr. Fr. Fritzsche und D. Strauss," TSuK, 1842, XV, No. 3, pp. 701-05; "Noch ein Wort über die Persönlichkeit Christi und das Wunderbare in der evangelischen Geschichte," TSuK, 1838, Xl, No. 2, pp. 305-06.

[106] Kern, "Erörterung der Hauptthatsachen der evangelischen Geschichte," TZ, 1836, No. 2, pp. 27-31. cf. also: Alexander Schweizer, "Das Leben Jesu von Strauss, im Verhältnisse zur Schleiermacher'schen Dignität des Religionsstifters," TSuK, 1837, X, No. 3, p. 488.

[107] A. Ruge and Th. Echtermeyer edited the Hallische Jahrbücher für deutsche Wissenschaft und Kunst, which began publication in 1838 as the organ for the Younger Hegelian School.

[108] cf. C. H. Weisse, "Die philosophische Litteratur der Gegenwart," 2ter Artikel, Z für Ph, Vll, No. 1, pp. 103-13.

[109] cf.e.g., Hegel, On Art, Religion, Philosophy, pp. 165-71; The Philosophy of History, pp. 9-10.

[110] Weisse, "Strauss und Bruno Bauer, Eine kritische Parallele," Z für Ph, X, No. 1, pp. 44f.

[111] cf. Strauss's dissertation: *Die Lehre von der Wiederbringung aller Dinge in ihrer religionsgeschichtlichen Entwicklung* reprinted in Müller, *Identität und Immanenz*, pp. 50-81. The dissertation was written from the Hegelian standpoint and ascribes to this philosophy the correct solution to the restoration of all things. "Dass aber schon die Religion dem Geiste eine gegenwärtige Lösung aller Widersprüche seines fromen Bewusstseyns gebe-diess leugnet Hegel mit Recht, den viele Religiöse haben, wie wir eben sahen, jene Lösung in ferne Zukunft verschoben, und er schreibt diess der wahren Philosophie zu, welche demnach subjectiv betrachtet die Wiederbringung aller Dinge ist." (p. 81). (Hegel correctly denies that religion gives the spirit an actual resolution of all the contradictions of a pious consciousness. For, as we just saw, many religious people postpone that resolution to a distant future. Hegel ascribes it to the true philosophy which, considered subjectively, is, accordingly, the restoration of all things.)

[112] cf. recent critics of Strauss: *Hartlich and Sachs, Der Ursprung des Mythosbegriffes*, p. 147; Harris, *David Friedrich Strauss*, pp. 270f; Sandberger, *Strauss als theologischer Hegelianer*, pp. 100f.

[113] It is on this basis that Allwohn in *Der Mythos bei Schelling* contrasts the mythic concept in the thought of Strauss and that of Schelling. Strauss, Allwohn writes, "wanted to free the religious consciousness of mankind from mythology and lead it to a Christianity without myths. Therefore, he offered the concept of myth to eliminate the miraculous narratives in the New Testament. Automatically and without exception, the concept of myth acquired the mark of the historically untrue, a mark that is not found in Schellings's specifications of the concept even in the first period. In this connection, it again becomes clear with how little justification, Strauss, the radical opponent of myth, can be placed next to Schelling who in all his stages somehow remained a believer in myth." (p. 74)

[114] *LJ*, §144.

[115] Schweizer, "Das Leben Jesu von Strauss, im Verhältnisse zur Schleiermacher'schen Dignität des Religionstifters," TSuK, 1837, X, No. 3, pp. 494-96. Schweizer was prompted to write this article because of the relationship that was being proposed between Schleiermacher's theology and Strauss's Leben Jesu. In Schweizer's view the speculative presuppositions inherent in Strauss's Christology, far from being in agreement with Schleiermacher's principles, were specifically directed against Schleiermacher. v., Schweizer, "Ueber die Dignität des Religionsstifters. Ein Beitrag zur Ausmittelung des Wesens der Frömmigkeit, TSuK, 1834, Vll, No. 3, pp. 521-70; No. 4, pp. 823-30.

[116] Ullmann, "Das Leben Jesu," TSuK, 1836, lX, No. 3, pp. 806-12; Fr. Vorländer, "Ueber die philosophisch-theologische Theorie des Dr. Strauss, Verfasser des Lebens Jesu," Z für Ph, lll, No. 1, p. 76.

[117] LJ, §148.

[118] Kern, "Erörterung der Hauptthatsachen der evangelischen Geschichte, in Rücksicht auf Strauss's Schrift: 'Das Leben Jesu,'" TZ, 1836, No. 2, pp. 20-34.

[119] Ullmann, "Polemisches in Betreff der Sündlosigkeit Jesu, mit besonderer Beziehung auf D. Chr. Fr. Fritzsche und D. Strauss," TSuK, 1842, XV, No. 3, pp. 706-10; "Noch ein Wort über die Persönlichkeit Christi und das Wunderbare in der evangelischen Geschichte," TSuK, Xl, 1838, No. 2, p. 300-10; "Ueber die Unsündlichkeit Jesu. Eine apologetische Betrachtung," TSuK, 1828, 1, No. 1, pp. 8-48. v. also Vorländer, "Ueber die philosophisch-theologische Theorie des Dr. Strauss, Verfasser des Lebens Jesu," Z für Ph, lll, No. 1, p. 76.

[120] Schenkel, "Ueber die neuesten Bearbeitungen des Lebens Jesu," TSuK, 1840, Xlll, No. 3, pp. 739f.

[121] Ullmann, "Das Leben Jesu," TSuK, 1836, lX, No. 3, p. 813; Vorländer, "Ueber die philosophisch-theologische Theorie des Dr. Strauss, Verfasser des Lebens Jesu," Z für Ph, lll, No. 1, p. 95. cf. also Schweizer, "Das Leben Jesu von Strauss im Verhältnisse zur Schleiermacher'schen Dignität des Religionsstifters," TSuK, 1837, X, No. 3, pp. 494f.; Kern, "Erörterung der Hauptthatsachen der evangelischen Geschichte, in Rücksicht auf Strauss's Schrift: 'Das Leben Jesu,'"TZ, 1836, No. 2, pp. 27-31.

[122] Kern, "Erörterung der Hauptthatsachen der evangelischen Geschichte," TZ, 1836, No. 2, pp. 22-23.

[123]Schweizer's connection between the inspired genius and the inspired founder of a religion was in keeping with the then current cult of the genius that also found its way into theology. In Ueber das Vergängliche und Bleibende im Christenthum, Strauss himself maintained that Christ belonged to the category of genius, for in him appeared the highest and purest genius of mankind, in which man knew himself one with God.

[124]Schweizer, "Das Leben Jesu von Strauss in Verhältnisse zur Schleiermacher'schen Dignität des Religionsstifters," TSuK, 1837, X, No. 3, pp 467-78.

[125]LJ, §148.

[126]Schweizer, "Das Leben Jesu von Strauss im Verhältnisse zur Schleiermacher'schen Dignität des Religionsstifters," TSuK, 1837, X, No. 3, pp. 478-84.

[127]Kern, "Erörterung der Hauptthatsachen der evangelischen Geschichte, in Rücksicht auf Strauss's Schrift: 'Das Leben Jesu,'" TZ, 1836, No. 2, p. 23; Vorländer, "Ueber die philosophisch-theologische Theorie des Dr. Strauss, Verfasser des Lebens Jesu," Z für Ph, 111, No. 1, pp. 80-84; Ullmann, "Polemisches in Betreff der Sündlosigkeit Jesu, mit besonderer Beziehung auf D. Chr. Fr. Fritzsche und D. Strauss," TSuK, 1842, XV, No. 3, pp. 643-44.

[128]LJ, §1.

[129]v. on causality and similarity: Vorländer, "Ueber die philosophisch-theologische Theorie des D. Strauss, Verfasser des Lebens Jesu," Z für Ph, 111, No. 1, p. 91; Schenkel, "Ueber die neuesten Bearbeitungen des Lebens Jesu," TSuK, 1840, XIII, No. 3, pp. 771f.; 783-86; Kern, "Erörterung der Hauptthatsachen der evangelischen Geschichte, in Rücksicht auf Strauss's Schrift: 'Das Leben Jesu,'" TZ, 1836, No. 2, pp. 105-06.

[130]J. Müller, "Bemerkung zum dritten Hefte der Streitschriften über das Leben Jesu von D. D. F. Strauss," TSuK, 1838, XI, No. 2, pp. 376-77.

[131]Kern, "Erörterung der Hauptthatsachen der evangelischen Geschichte, in Rücksicht auf Strauss's Schrift: 'Das Leben Jesu,'" TZ, 1836, No. 2, pp. 105-06; 1838, No. 1, pp. 105-10; 1839, No. 2, p. 1-45; Ullmann, "Noch ein Wort über die Persönlichkeit Christi und das Wunderbare," TSuK, 1838, XI, No. 2,

pp. 324-25; Müller, "Das Leben Jesu," TSuK, 1836, IX, No. 3, p. 822; C. L. Nitzsch, "Theologische Beantwortung der philosophischen Dogmatik des D. D. F. Strauss," 3ter Artikel, TSuK, 1843, XVI, No. 1, pp. 36-45.

[132]On the discussion of the problems perceived in connection with Strauss's application of his myth concept and of the attempts to refine the concept of myth, cf.: Ullmann, "Noch ein Wort über die Persönlichkeit Christi und das Wunderbare in der evangelischen Geschichte," TSuK, 1838, XI, No. 2, pp. 293-352; Das Leben Jesu," TSuK, 1836, IX, No. 3, pp. 787-806. The former article was written in response to Strauss's third Streitschrift which was directed against Ullmann. Ullmann, "Polemisches in Betreff der Sündlosigkeit Jesu," TSuK, 1842, XV, No. 3, pp. 684-88. This article was simultaneously an announcement of the fourth edition of Ullmann's work on the sinlessness of Jesus, in which Ullmann did not include polemics in order to avoid having the work become too unwiedly. Ullmann stated that he had not wanted to deal with Strauss because he did not want polemics against Strauss to be included in the articles of his literary activity. He could not avoid Strauss, however, because the nature of the latter's work would not permit it. (p. 641); C. H. Weisse, "Ueber den Begriff des Mythus und seine Anwendung auf die neutestamentliche Geschichte," Z für Ph, IV, No. 1, pp. 83-102; IV, No. 2, pp. 216-54; V, No. 1, pp. 114-54; "Strauss und Bruno Bauer," Z für Ph, X, No. 1, pp. 41-42; Kern, "Erörterung der Hauptthatsachen der evangelischen Geschichte, TZ, 1838, No. 2, pp. 92-165; Schenkel, "Ueber die neuesten Bearbeitungen des Lebens Jesu," TSuK, 1840, Xlll, No. 3, pp. 775-76; Steudel, "Vorläufig zu Beherzigendes, TZ, 1837, No. 2, pp. 56-59; J. Müller, "Bemerkung zum dritten Hefte der Streitschriften," TSuK, 1838, Xl, No. 2, pp. 377-79; "Das Leben Jesu," TSuK, 1836, IX, No. 3, pp. 839-84.

[133]The terms world-historical, world-conquering, and world-forming were used in reference to Christ's consciousness and the effects proceeding from this consciousness by Ullmann. cf., e.g., Ullman, "Noch ein Wort über die Persönlichkeit Christi and das Wunderbare in der evangelischen Geschichte," TSuK, 1838, Xl, No. 2, pp. 293-98.

[134]LJ, p. 742. §140.

[135]Recent studies on Midrash support this approach. cf., e.g., Herford, Christianity in Talmud and Midrash; Block, Midrash; and Drury, Tradition & Design in Luke's Gospel.

[136]Kern, "Erörterung der Hauptthatsachen der evangelischen Geschichte," TZ, 1838, No. 2, pp. 96-98.

[137]ibid., pp. 119-25. With this insight Strauss anticipates redaction criticism. cf., e.g., Braatan & Harrisville, The Historical Jesus and the Kerygmatic Christ.

[138]Geier, "Die Alexander-Mythen verglichen mit den sogenannten Evangelischen Mythen. Ein Beitrag zur Kritik über die Schrift von Strauss: 'Das Leben Jesu,'" Z für h Th, 1838, Vlll, No. 3, pp. 119-58.

[139]Weisse, Review of A. Tholuck's Die Glaubwürdigkeit der evangelischen Geschichte, Z für Ph, 1837, No. 2, pp. 262-67.

Bibliography

Primary Sources

Hegel, G.W.F. Early Theological Writings. Translated by T.M. Knox. Phila.: University of Pennsylvania Press, 1971.

_____. On Art, Religion, Philosophy. Edited and introduced by J. Glenn Gray. New York & Evanston: Harper & Row, 1970.

_____. The Essential Writings. Edited and introduced by Frederich G. Weiss. New York: Harper & Row, 1974.

_____. The Phenomenology of Mind. Translated and introduced by J.B. Baillie. New York & Evanston: Harper & Row, 1967.

_____. The Philosophy of History. Introduction by C.C. Friedrich. New York: Dover Publications, Inc., 1956.

Kant, Immanuel. Critique of Practical Reason. Translated by Lewis White Peck. Indianapolis: Bobbs-Merrill Co., Inc., 1975.

_____. Critique of Pure Reason. Translated by Norman Kemp Smith. New York: St. Martin's Press, 1965.

Strauss, David Friedrich. Ausgewählte Briefe von David Friedrich Strauss. Edited by Eduard Zeller. Bonn: Emil Strauss, 1895.

_____. Der Christus des Glaubens und der Jesu der Geschichte. Edited by Hans-Jürgen Geischer. Gütersloh: Gerd Mohn, 1971.

_____. Gesammelte Schriften. Edited by Eduard Zeller. Vol. 10: Christian Märklin.

_____. Gesammelte Schriften. Edited by Eduard Zeller. Vol. 6: Der alte und der neue Glaube. Bonn: Emil Strauss, 1877.

_____. Gesammelte Schriften. Edited by Eduard Zeller. Vol. 1: Justinus Kerner. Bonn: Emil Strauss, 1877.

_____. *Gesammelte Schriften*. Edited by Eduard Zeller. Vol. 1: *Literarische Denkwürdigkeiten*. Bonn: Emil Strauss, 1877.

_____. *Streitschriften zur Vertheidigung meiner Schrift über das Leben Jesu und zur Charakteristik der gegenwärtigen Theologie*. Tübingen: C.F. Osiander, 1838.

_____. *The Life of Jesus Critically Examined*. Edited by Peter C. Hodgson. Translated by George Eliot. Phila.: Fortress Press, 1972

_____. *Gesammelte Schriften*. Edited by Eduard Zeller. Vol. 1: *Zum Andenken an meine gute Mutter*. Bonn: Emil Strauss, 1877.

Journal Articles

Beck, Johann Tobias. "Ueber mythische Auffassung der neutestamentlichen Evangelien-Urkunden, ein Beitrag zu deren theologischen Würdigung," *TZ*, 1835, VII, No. 4, pp. 63-80.

"Brief des 18. Dez., 1841," *Z für h Th*, 1841, XI, No. 4, pp. 180-82.

Dettinger, M. "Der Seelenkampf Jesu in Gethsemane. Ein theologischer Versuch mit besonderer Rücksicht auf die Strauss'sche Kritik," *TZ*, 1837, IX, No. 4, pp. 135-46; 1838, X, No. 3, pp. 94-116.

"Der Kampf der Principien im Canton Zürich im Jahre 1839," *Z für h Th.*, 1840, X, No. 3, pp. 94-116.

de Wette, Wilhelm Martin Leberecht. "Eine Bemerkung über die von Herrn Dr. Steudel in Tübinger aufgeworfene Frage (in der Tübinger Zeitschrift, 1 St., S. 74): 'Ueber die Ausführbarkeit einer Annäherung zwischen der rationalistischen und supranaturalistischen Ansicht,'" *TSuK*, 1828, 1, No. 3, pp. 563-67.

"Die verschiedenen Rücksichten, in welchen und fur welche der Biograph Jesu arbeiten kann," *Krit. Journal*, V, No. 3, pp. 225-45.

Gabler, Johann Philipp. "Ist es erlaubt in der Bibel und sogar im Neuen Testamente Mythen anzunehmen?" *J f a th Lit*, 11, No. 1, pp. 43-53.

Geier, Samuel Robert. "Die Alexander-Mythen verglichen mit den sogenannten Evengelischen Mythen. Ein Beitrag zur Kritik über die Schrift von Strauss: Das Leben Jesu," Z f h Th, 1838, VIII, No. 3, pp. 119-58.

Gelpke, Ernst Friedrich. "Ueber den richtigen Standpunct einer Kritik der evangelischen Geschichte," Z für Ph, IV, No. 2, pp. 255-90.

Göss, Carl Georg Friedrich. "Der Mysticismus, eignet er sich nach der Behauptung seiner Anwälde zur vesten Burg der religiösen und kirchlichen Interessen?" Krit. Journal, XIII, No. 1, pp. 1-32,

Hahn, August. "Für grammatisch-historische Interpretation und gegen traditionelle, philosophische und allegorische. Ein vorläufiger Versuch," TSuK, 1830, III, No. 2, pp. 301-30.

Hanne, W. "Beiträge zur Charakteristik und Kritik der gegenwärtigen religiösen Zeitrichtungen. In Briefen an einen Freund," Z für Ph, XV, No. 2, pp. 249-81.

Kern, Heinrich. "Erörterung der Hauptthatsachen der evangelischen Geschichte, in Rücksicht auf Strauss's Schrift: 'Das Leben Jesu,'" TZ, 1836, No. 2, pp. 14-102; 1836, No. 3, pp. 3-59; 1838 No. 2, pp. 3-175; 1839, No. 1, pp. 105-90; 1839, No. 2, pp. 2-54.

Müller, Julius. "Bemerkung zum dritten Hefte der Streitschriften über das Leben Jesu von D. D.F. Strauss," TSuK, 1838, XI, No. 2, pp.370-83.

_____. "Das Leben Jesu," TSuK, 1836, IX, No. 3, pp. 813-90.

_____. Review of Ch. H. Weisse's Review of Richter: Die Lehre von den letzten Dingen," TSuK, 1835, VIII, No. 3, pp. 703-94.

Nitzsch, Carl Ludwig. "Eine theologische Beantwortung der philosophischen Dogmatik der D. D. F. Strauss," TSuK, 1842, XV, No. 1, pp. 1-51; 1842, XV, No. 3, pp. 605-39; 1843, XVl, No. 1, pp.36-60; 1843, XVl, No. 2, pp. 378-415.

Osiander, J.C. "Apologie des Lebens Jesu gegen den neuesten Versuch, es in Mythen aufzulösen," TZ, 1836, No. 4, pp. 33-202; 1837, No. 1, pp. 3 -238.

Quinet, Edgar. "Ueber das Leben Jesu von Dr. Strauss," Translated by O. Schwab. Excerpts from Revue des deux Mondes, Dec. 1838, TZ, 1839, No. 4, pp. 1-27.

Schenkel, Daniel. "Ueber die neuesten Bearbeitung des Lebens Jesu," TSuK, 1840, XIII, No. 3, pp. 736-807.

Schweizer, Alexander. "Das Leben Jesu von Strauss, im Verhältniss zur Schleiermacherschen Dignität des Religionsstifters," TSuK, 1837, X, No. 3, pp. 458-510.

_____. "Ueber die Dignität des Religionsstifters. Ein Beitrag zur Ausmittelung des Wesens der Frömmigkeit," TSuK, 1834, VII, No. 3, pp. 521-71; 1834, VII, No. 4, pp. 813-49.

_____. "Zur Verständigung über die aufgeregte Stimmung in Deutschland," TSuK, 1846, XIX, No. 2, pp. 491-516.

Sengler, "Ueber die gegenwärtige Zeit und wie sie geworden ist," Z für Ph, VII, No. 1, pp. 1-25.

Stäudlin, Carl Friedrich. "Ueber die blos historische Auslegung der Bucher des Neuen Testaments," Krit. Journal, 1, No. 4, pp. 321-48; 11, No. 1, pp. 1-39; 11, No. 1, pp, 113-47,

Steudel, Johann Christian Friedrich. "Die Frage uber die Ausfuhrbarkeit einer Annaherung zwischen der rationalistischen und supranaturalistischen Ansicht, mit besonderer Rucksicht auf den Standpunkt der Schleiermacher'schen Glaubenslehre," TZ, 1828, 1, No. 1, pp. 74-199; 1, No. 2, pp. 74-120.

_____. "Erwiderung auf eine Bemerkung des Herrn Dr. de Wette in den theologischen Studien und Kritiken, Bd. 1, Heft 3, pp. 563ff." TSuK, 1829, 11, No. 1, pp. 127-37.

_____. "Kurzer Bescheid auf Hrn. D. David Fried. Straussens Streitschriften, Heft 1," TZ, No. 2, pp. 119-84.

_____. "Vorläufig zu Beherzigendes," TZ, 1835, No. 3, pp. 17-99.

_____. "Ueber das bei alleiniger Anerkennung des historischen Christus sich für die Bildung des Glaubens ergebende Verfahren. Sendschreiben D. Steudels an Hrn. D. Schleiermacher," TZ, 1830, 11, No. 1, pp. 1-48.

_____. "Ueber das Leben Jesu von Strauss, in der Foreign quarterly review," TZ, 1839, XI, No. 4, pp. 32-46.

Ullmann, Carl. "Das Leben Jesu," TSuK, 1836, IX, No. 3, pp. 770-813.

_____. "Das Wesen des Christenthums, mit Beziehung auf neuere Auffassungsweisen desselben von Freunden und Gegnern," TSuK, 1849, XXII, No. 4, pp. 961-66.

_____. "Noch ein Wort über die Persönlichkeit Christi und das Wunderbare in der evangelischen Geschichte," TSuK, 1838, XI, No. 2, pp. 277-369.

_____. "Polemisches in Betreff der Sündlosigkeit Jesu, mit besonderer Beziehung auf D. Chr. Fr. Fritzsche und D. Strauss," TSuK, 1841, XV, No. 3, pp. 640-710.

_____. "Theologische Aphorismen," TSuK, 1835, VIII, No. 2, pp. 539-616; 1835, VIII, No. 4, pp. 955-63; 1844, XVII, No. 1, pp. 157-85; 1844, XVII, No. 2, pp. 417-54; 1845, XVIII, No. 3, pp. 665-84.

_____. "Ueber den unterscheidenden Charakter des Christenthums, mit Beziehung auf neuere Auffassungsweisen," TSuK, 1845, XVIII, No. 1, pp. 7-61.

_____. "Ueber die Unsündlichkeit Jesu, Eine apologetische Betrachung," TSuK, 1828, 1, No. 1, pp. 3-83.

Ulrici, Hermann. "Aphorismen zur philosophischen Verständigung über die Tendenzen unserer Zeit," Z für Ph, XVII, No. 1, pp. 25-36; XVII, No. 2, pp. 208-26.

Usteri, Leonard. "Beitrag zur Erklärung der Versuchungsgeschichte," TSuK, 1832, V, No. 4, pp. 768-91.

Vorländer, Friedrich, "Ueber die philosophisch-theologische Theorie des Dr. Strauss, Verfasser des Lebens Jesu," Z für Ph, 111, No. 1, pp. 69-100.

Weisse, Christian Hermann. "Die geschichtlichen Voraussetzungen der Straussischen Glaubenslehre," Z für h Th, 1842, XIII, No. 3, pp. 101-79.

_____. "Die philosophische Litteratur der Gegenwart," Z für Ph, VI, No. 2, pp. 269-303; VIII, No. 1, pp. 103-49.

_____. Review: A. Tholuck: Die Glaubwürdigkeit der evangelischen Geschichte, Z für ph, 1837, 1, No. 2, pp. 259-300.

_____. "Strauss und Bruno Bauer. Eine kritische Parallele," Z für Ph, X, No. 1, pp. 40-82.

_____. "Ueber das Verhältniss der Glaubenslehre zur Philosophie. Mit Beziehung auf Schleiermacher und andere Zeiterscheinungen," Z für Ph, XVI, No. 1, pp. 1-39.

_____. "Ueber den Begriff des Mythus und seine Anwendung auf die neutestamentliche Geschichte," Z für Ph, IV, No. 1, pp. 74-102; IV, No. 2, pp. 215-54; V, No. 1, pp. 114-54.

Secondary Sources

Allwohn, Adolf. Der Mythos bei Schelling. Kant Studien #61. Charlottenburg: Pan-Verlag Rolf Heise, 1927.

Anderson, Charles C. The Historical Jesus: A Continuing Quest. Grand Rapids: William B. Eerdmans, 1972.

Backhaus, Gunther. Kerygma und Mythos bei David Friedrich Strauss und Rudolf Bultmann. Hamburg-Bergstedt: Herbert Reich Evangelischer Verlag, G.m.b.H., 1956.

Barth, Karl. David Friedrich Strauss als Theologe 1839-1939. Theologische Studien #6. Zürich: Verlag der Evangelischen Buchhandlung Zollikon, 1939.

_____. Die protestantische Theologie im 19. Jahrhundert: ihre Vorgeschichte und ihre Geschichte. Zollikon Zürich: Evangelischer Verlag, 1947.

Bloch, Renèe. "Midrash." Dictionnaire de la Bible. Supplement V. cols. 1263-81.

Cromwell, Richard S. David Friedrich Strauss and His Place in Modern Thought. Fair Lawn, New Jersey: R.E. Burdick, Inc., 1974.

Drury, John. Tradition and Design in Luke's Gospel: A Study in Early Christian Historiography. London: Darton, Longman and Todd Ltd., 1976.

Frei, Hans W. The Eclipse of Biblical Narrative. A Study in Eighteenth and Nineteenth Century Hermenentics. New Haven and London: Yale University Press, 1974.

Harnach, Adolf v. Das Wesen des Christentums. Leipzig: J. C. Hinrichs'sche Buchlandlung, 1933.

Harris, Horton. David Friedrich Strauss and His Theology. Cambridge: The University Press, 1973.

Hartlich, Christian and Sachs, Walter. Der Ursprung des Mythosbegriffes in der modernen Bibelwissenschaft. Tübingen: J. C. B. Mohr (Paul Siebick), 1952.

Hausrath, A. David Friedrich Strauss und die Theologie seiner Zeit. 2 vols. Heidelberg: Fr. Bassermann, 1876, 1878.

Herford, Robert Travers. Christianity in Talmud and Midrash. Clifton, New Jersey: Reference Book Publishers, 1966.

Kähler, Martin. The So-called Historical Jesus and the Historic, Biblical Christ. Translated and edited by Charles E. Braaten. Phila.: Fortress Press, 1970.

Kee, Howard Clark. Jesus in History: An Approach to the Study of the Gospels. New York: Harcourt, Brace and World, Inc., 1970.

Löwith, Karl. From Hegel to Nietzsche. The Revolution in Nineteenth-Century Thought. Translated by David E. Green. Garden City, New York: Doubleday and Co., Inc. 1967.

Müller, Gotthold. Identität und Immanenz: Zur Genese der Theologie von David Friedrich Strauss: Zürich, EVZ Verlag, 1968.

Nietzsche, Friedrich. Unzeitgemässe Betrachtungen: David Strauss, der Bekenner und der Schriftsteller. Stuttgart: Alfred Kröner, 1964.

Ryan, Michael Daniel. The Role of the Discipline of History in the Theological Interpretation of Albrecht Ritschl. Diss. Drew University, 1967.

Sandberger, Jörg F. David Friedrich Strauss als theologischer Hegelianer: Mit unveröffentlichten Briefen. Göttingen: Vanderhoeck u. Ruprecht. 1972.

Schweitzer, Albert. The Quest of the Historical Jesus. A Critical Study of its Progress from Reimarus to Wrede. London: A and C Black, 1922.

*The Historical Jesus and the Kerygmatic Christ. Essays on the New Quest of the Historical Jesus*. Edited and translated by Braaten, Carl E. and Harrisville, Roy A. New York and Nashville: Abingdon Press, 1975.

Welch, Claude, *Protestant Thought in the Nineteenth Century, Vol. 1, 1799-1870*. New Haven and London: Yale University Press, 1974.

Zeller, Eduard. *David Friedrich Strauss in his Life and Writings*. Authorized Translation. London: Smith, Elder and Co., 1874.

Ziegler, Theobald. *David Friedrich Strauss*. 2 vols. Strassburg: Karl J. Trübner, 1908.

# INDEX

Absoluteness of religion, 52, 80-86, 100
Archetype, problem of, 78-89, 94

Bauer, Georg Lorenz, 30, 34
Baur, Ferdinand Christian, 3, 10, 33-34
Beck, Johann Tobias, 3, 58-59
Boehme, Jacob, 11, 17

Concept (BEGRIFF), 14-15, 71-78 v. also Representation

Development, problem of, 89-93; v. also Archetype
de Wette, Wilhelm Martin Leberecht, 3, 31-33, 99

Eichhorn, Johann Gottfried, 24-28, 34

Gabler, Johann Philipp, 3, 24-30, 34
Geier, Samuel Robert, 3-4, 109
Gelpke, Ernst Friedrich, 4, 56-58

Hahn, August, 4
Hegel, Friedrich, 13-15, 17 66-78
Heyne, Christian Gottlob, 23-24, 25, 28

Kant, Immanuel, 1, 10-11, 13, 79, 92
Kern, Heinrich, 4, 10, 70, 83-85, 89, 96-97

Marheinike, Philipp Konrad, 13, 72
Miracles, 84, 94-98
Mueller, Julius, 4, 67, 71, 96
Myth, sources of Strauss's concept of, 21-39; Strauss's concept of, 42-45, 104-105; criticism of, 99-110

Mythic School, 23-33
Mythic Principle, 34-39

Older Hegelian School, 71-73

Pantheism, 88-89

Quinet, Edgar, 4

Representation (VOR-STELLUNG), 14-15, 71-78; v. also Concept

Schelling, Friedrich, 10, 11, 12, 17, 133n113
Schenkel, Daniel, 4, 66-67, 71, 88-89
Schleiermacher, Friedrich Ernst Daniel, 11-12, 13, 15, 18, 71, 81, 92, 134n115
Schweizer, Alexander, 4, 67, 80-82, 90-93, 134n 115
Sinlessness, 83-86, 94
Staeudlin, Carl Friedrich, 4, 54-55
Steudel, Johann Christian Friedrich, 4-5, 53-54, 97
Strauss, Christiane, 9-10
Strauss, David Friedrich, 7-19; works, DAS LEBEN JESU, 15, 18, 39-45, 128n63; as destructive criticism, 46-50; DER ALTE UND DER NEUE GLAUBE, 17, 18; DIE LEHRE VON DER WIEDERBRINGUNG ALLER DINGE IN IHRER RELIGIONS-GESCHICHTLICHEN ENTWICKLUNG, 133n111; UEBER DAS VERGAENGLICHE UND BLEIBENDE IM CHRISTENTHUM, 134n123
Strauss, Georgine, 16
Strauss, Johann Friedrich, 9-10
Strauss, Wilhelm, 18

Tuebingen School, 10

Ullmann, Carl, 5, 59-62,
  66, 70-71, 82, 85-86, 89,
  96, 136n132
Usteri, Leonard, 5, 38-39, 99

Vatke, W., 39

Vorlaender, Friedrich, 5, 67,
  71, 82, 89

Weisse, Christian Hermann,
  5, 72, 74-76, 109-110

Younger Hegelian School,
  71-73

## Appendix

Anon, "The Various Considerations From Which and For Which the Biographer of Jesus Can Work," <u>Kritisches Journal</u>, V, 3, 1816, pp. 225-45.

The evangelic story, which many had already attempted to write at the time of Luke, has always found and still finds the most varied revisers. And it is not easy to reject anyone of them as a totally incompetent narrator of what has often been narrated. A fusion of incentives which does not occur in such a way with any other object in the world accounts for this. If the recent revisions of this story are to be properly appreciated and if at the same time the unique essence of the biblical story in general and the evangelic story in particular is to be discussed in this journal, then it might be useful to put forth beforehand the various considerations from which and for which the biographer of Jesus can work. This will not only anticipate and ease the criticism that follows but will also indirectly exemplify it. We find these various considerations partly in the high interest which this story has; partly in the diversity of the readers for whom it can be revised; partly in the diversity of views from which it can be revised; and partly in the various modes of treatment which this very flexible material permits.

I. The evangelic story has a two-fold interest: a purely historical one and a dogmatic one. Regardless of the contemporary voices that may be raised against this opinion, in Christianity the history and teaching of Christ are closely connected with each other not only because the former contains the genesis of the latter and together with it often contains the psychological reasons for the latter but primarily because Christ is not merely the subject but also the object of the teaching, not merely the proclaimer of salvation but the salvation itself that is being offered to believers. He says that eternal life is the recognition of Jesus Christ Who alone is the true God and Whom God has sent. Thus, if we cannot separate the history of Jesus from Christianity, then that distinction between Christians in the broad and narrow sense of the word which a reviewer in the J. A. L. Z. recently wanted to posit is pure nonsense. Those who are supposed to accept the teachings of Christianity which can exist and be recognized without reference to the teacher might be thought of as pious pagans; they are not, however, Christians who do not deny the positive character of the teaching which is grounded in history: for Christianity does not consist only of moral principles but also in theorems which serve as the foundation for the former. Just as the history reaches over into the teaching so, too, is it unavoidable that the teaching must effect the history or at least give it a very particular interest. Thus, we assume a two-fold interest:

A. a purely historical interest which is concerned solely with the teacher, His personality and His deeds. It creates for us the history of a man who accomplished in a definite time, at a definite place, and under definite circumstances something which the world and posterity has admired as great and good. This interest will claim all the aides of criticism, of the study of the age, the people and the country, of the language, etc. and will psychologically prove what follows as grounded in what preceded. This purely historical interest leaves the decision as to whether what happened occurred miraculously or naturally to further philosophical discussions and is satisfied with knowing <u>what</u> happened. This story, however, also has:

B. a dogmatic interest where the great teacher appears as the Eternal Word which elevated over all time, nonetheless, appeared in the form of time and space since it became flesh. Elevated above everything human, He became mere man in order to become the Redeemer of the human race. He, therefore, cannot be seen and judged as a product of time, His teaching is not the sole, indeed not the highest, purpose of His earthly life: He Himself is. He is the Lamb of God, Who takes away the sins of the world; God is in Him and reconciled the world with Himself. His teaching is only an indication as to how we should embrace the salvation offered in Him. In this respect Christ is not the object of historical research but solely of pious belief. For him whom this interest inspires history becomes only the outer shell, only the skin of a more beautiful fruit. In order to grasp the variety of revisions we look at:

II. the infinite diversity of the readers to whom the evangelic story is supposed to be offered. The story of a founder of a religion who for almost 2,000 years has become for the minds and hearts of humankind wisdom, justice, salvation and redemption must be important. In this respect, however, these people can be divided:

    A.  according to the degree of their education into

        1.  the learned

            a.  theologians

                i.  educated researchers
              ii.  popular teachers

            b.  non-theologians

        2.  the unlearned

            a.  cultured

            b.  uncultured

                i.  adults

                      a.  reflective
                      b.  crude

                ii.  children

    B.  according to the religious sense into

        1.  believers

            a.  fanatical and hyperorthodox
            b.  critical

2. non-believers
    a. doubters
    b. scorners

Naturally the story claims to be shaped differently for each class of these readers. And we understand how a Gr. von Stollberg and the author of the natural history of the great prophet of Nazareth, how a Herder and Hess, a Meister and Greiling, a Federsen and Wilmsen and many others can coexist and find their public.

More important and in part founded in the above, in part derived from the peculiar nature of the sources is:

III. the diversity of the point of view from which this story can be seen; for here it appears either as true and pure history or as myth or as a blend of the two.

A. The purely historical point of view lets us see it as miraculous history or natural history.

1. The old believers and the orthodox believers up until the present day saw it as <u>miraculous history</u>. They remained by the letter of the document and the entire story, even where easily comprehended, is a miracle for them, for it is the hero of the story. They must necessarily decline the usual standard of credibility; through steady consistency their opinion attains a posture to which respect cannot at all be denied. A very respected following of scholars and believers, equipped with a highly significant apparatus of scholarship and discernment, fight for this view.

2. It can also be seen as natural history. Stripped of everything miraculous, events are everywhere seen as brought about by the natural course of events. Therefore, this view in part eliminates the incomprehensible and/or in part makes it comprehensible through conjectures or additions. If one does not want to fault the shortsightedness or fidelity of the writers, the obscurities and apparent miracles are attributed to the brevity of the presentation, to unfamiliarity with time, people, land, and languages. If this natural history is to be carried out consistently, then, overburdened with a host of caprices, it must necessarily extract the holy and divine and be degraded to a vain novel which only usurped the name of history. What primarily opposes this view is:

a) the completely unhistorical procedure which allows itself to augment documents with suppositions and takes speculations for literalness. No old storyteller is as mistreated as is the Bible; one does not force our belief on Herodotus and does not expect from Livius that he should withdraw his _portenta_ to please our taste. The historical researcher must remain with what historical interpretation has given grammatically; there is no _plus_ _ultra_. History and fiction are in open confrontation.

b) to portray naturally what the documents gave as something miraculous results in an effort which is often extremely forced and always inconceivable. Since the Wolfenbuettel fragmentist, Barth, Eck, the author of the letters about the

Bible, etc. began to throw doubt on the credibility of miraculous history and to substitute natural explanations, one has thought to be able to save the honor of the Bible best through clear explanations of everything that happened in the evangelic story. This was done to flatter the spirit of an age that wanted to see everything clearly. The ingenuity of the most practiced interpreters was directed to that end; even those who earlier forged the path for a mythical treatment were inclined, ut dicunt, to the factual explanation. And one may assume that this effort culminates in Paulus' commentary. One can suspect that this effort often contrasts most strangely with all probability and with all laws of language and thought. We will demonstrate it more below when we have to accuse Mr. Greiling of this procedure. Instead of all other examples we mention here only the most eloquent, viz., the resurrection and ascension. The resurrection is considered a reawakening from an apparent death, and the ascension, a disappearance on the Mt. of Olives which was heavily covered by clouds. Gruner showed: "de morte Jesu Christi vera, non synoptica" how improbable the former was in a way which the theologian might scarcely be able to oppose. If, in addition, we take the entire life of Jesus after His resurrection as the Evangelists present it: His spirit-like appearances; the 40 days of His new stay on earth (Moses fasted 40 days on Sinai, Jesus fasted 40 days in the desert, the Jewish criminal received 40 lashes, the Jewess remained for 40 days in confinement); what was left unfinished in the reunion; what is aphoristic in the part of the story which must be the best known to all; and finally the supralunar figures who play their roles in the resurrection and ascension, and combine it with the vital wish to be able to vindicate for the hero of the story this greatest of all miracles, then it seems much more natural to cover the fact with the mythic husk than to act contrary to the clear letter of the Evangelists by trying to make it comprehensible.

c) It is a bad deception if one thinks that the dignity of the Bible and religiosity win thereby. Nothing has been more disadvantageous to the dignity of the Bible and the respect due it than precisely this arbitrariness with which it has been treated. And it could not be otherwise. If every authorized and unauthorized interpreter can impose his favorite view on the Evangelists, if one questions their honesty or seeks to save them at the cost of their understanding, if the results are just as diverse and contradictory as are the paths to attain these results, if, in a word, one may jump about with the Bible, its authors and its content as one will: how can respect for such a book exist? The effort to illuminate everything and the trivialities and farces which one thinks to recognize in this light must repress all religiousness which, we freely admit, grows much better in a certain half-darkness. <u>Manum de tabula</u>! The sacred wants to be grasped alive and whole; the anatomical knife is only for cadavers. If by means of this explaining of what appears to be incomprehensible one was convinced of having opened a further field for popular instruction, this is just as deceptive: the practical usefulness of historical texts rests on the fact that the historical is clearly grounded in the document. Often it might, therefore, be much more purposeful to allegorize such texts in which the practical remains independent of the truth of history. Compare Tzschirner's <u>Memorabilia</u> V, 1., p. 47f. We now come:

B. to the mythical point of view which leaves the material of the narrative undisputed and does not dare to twist or subtilize anything in it. In this viewpoint the whole is not true history but holy saga. This view does not deny that some true event may be basic to many of the reports, but it does not want to strip the actual from the mythic guise in which it sees it concealed, doubtful as to how much belongs to the former, how much to the latter. Even the mediating way proposed by Gabler in the <u>Neues Theologische Journal</u>, V. 7, p. 386f., does not seem necessary to us. This ingenious scholar wants to have the division into historical and philosophical myths (i.e., those for which either a fact or an idea is fundamental) which was proposed for primitive history applied to the history of the New Testament. We deem it more advisable to refrain totally from all judgment about the origin of individual myths since attempts at explanation must necessarily be just as precarious and uncertain here as Voss, so it seems to us, sufficiently demonstrated in his mythological letters about the explanations of Greek myths that are peculiar to Heyne's School. The following remarks speak for this mythic view which if we want to continue to build consistently on what Gabler, de Wette, and others have done and shown with respect to the Old Testament must become the general view.

   a) The analogy with the entire political and religious antiquity, <u>Datur</u> <u>haec</u> <u>venia</u> <u>antiquitate</u> (says Livius) <u>ut miscendo humana divinis primordia urbium</u> (and even more divine worships) <u>angustiora faciat</u>. What is true of secular antiquity no one any longer desires to deny of the Old Testament narrative. If then it can be shown that the New Testament narratives are as similar to the myths of secular and sacred antiquity as one egg to another, should we not be justified in also considering them myths? In order to indicate at least the proof that we cannot demonstrate here, we will call attention only to a few similarities in which the secular and the Old Testament myth strikingly coincide with the evangelic story. When Jesus is born to a virgin without the compliance of a man, who does not think of Hercules, the Dioscuri, Romulus, Alexander, and others? Who does not think of that virgin in the middle most tower of Belus' Temple who according to Herodotus gave birth to the Babylonian priests? To whom should it not occur that also in the Old Testament notable men are always born of such mothers who would not have had children according to the natural course of events, e.g., Isaac, Simson, Samuel, John. The Old Testament prophets can be compared with Jesus in many respects, true types which the biblical history copied. In the case of Elijah and Jesus, namely, there is much that is conspicuously similar. If it is a myth in the case of Elijah, must it not also be a myth in the case of

Jesus? Elijah awakens the son of the Sunamite (II Kings 4); Jesus awakens the young man at Nain, the daughter of Jairi and Lazarus. Elijah feeds 100 people with little bread and blesses the oil jug of the widow; Jesus feeds 6,000 people (II Kings 4; John 6, Mark 8). Elijah and Jesus cure lepers; both go through water (II Kings 4; Matt. 14:25; concerning ἐπὶ θαλάσσης see below); both blind those sent out against them (II Kings 6:18; John 18:6); both have a host of invisible protectors (II Kings 6:17; Matt. 26:5; 4:11; Luke 22:43). Another prophet, Elias, ascends into heaven alive. Elijah watches him; so too, Jesus and His Apostles (II Kings 2:12; Acts 1:9.10). Who fails to recognize the same spirit! Jesus cannot be inferior to the miracle workers of the Old Testament. In the same spirit the legends of Christian antiquity are joined to the myths of the founding in that they ascribe all miraculous deeds and events of the evangelic story to the holy ones. Indeed, just as the follower continuously makes additions, so the legends not only have Mary ascend to heaven alive (like Aenoch, Elias, Jesus, and Romulus earlier; see Jacot de Voragine <u>Legenda</u>) but have her small house carried to Loretto; allow not only persons but also things belonging to them (relics) to perform miracles. And thus the sacred saga goes through all ages, up to the toothpick for toothaches which was constructed from Luther's deathbed spot and the patches from his often repaired coat which was sold as a cure for epilepsy.

b) With this view the numerous difficulties in the biblical story, which certainly are never to be resolved, disappear since myth derides all criticism. Who is unaware that the biblical story considered as history offers an abundance of such difficulties? Even time calculations, however much Bengel, Hess, Paulus, Greiling, and others concerned themselves with them, will not permit of construction since there is always one more of the beloved Easter feasts than is desired. Still more difficult is the attempted harmony among the four Gospel writers where something which was unknown or seemed extremely unimportant to one author was elaborately expounded upon by another; where one obviously narrates differently than the other. John and Matthew (if the first two chapters of the latter are not authentic) know nothing about either the birth or ascension of Jesus; only Luke, who was not an Apostle but collected from rumors and writings, knows these miraculous things. If, on the other hand, chapters one and two of Matthew are genuine, then one cannot comprehend why the zealous compiler Luke knows absolutely nothing about their important content. The several statements about a higher nature in Christ are totally the property of the apocalyptic John. Mark, on the other hand, as Griesbach has incontestably shown, has nothing of his own, thus, also no importance. Why this diversity if it is undisputed history? How natural, on the other hand, if it is sacred saga (truth and fiction from the life of Jesus) which tends not to test time and place and connection like the subsequent critic. One does not need the sword of Alexander to cut the knot asunder; rather we do not see this knot which the historical view alone has tied. All the hypotheses which in trying to solve difficulties only increase them fall; and the investigations into an original Gospel which have set into motion so many heads and pens become superfluous. By original Gospel one would have to understand with the reviewer of Schuetzen's diss. critica: <u>de evangeliis, quae ante evangelia canonica in ecclesia fuisse dicuntur</u> (A. L. Z. 1838, No. 105-06) the saga which already was in many a mouth before its written record. There may have been and probably must have been such an oral saga, however much also Fritzsche (<u>On the Authenticity of the Books of Moses, with an appendix on the Original Gospel</u>, Leipzig, 1814) contests this hypothesis. Only one must not take the agreement of the original and the copies so seriously since also the former can have appeared in very different physiognomies.

c) With the mythic husk the objectionable in the life of Jesus is removed from closer investigation. Here I especially mean what theologians have called accommodations to popular concepts, to concepts of time, and to the sophistic wisdom of Jesus. For me something totally different seems to be involved here. To be sure, I freely admit that, e.g., the popular belief in possession by the devil, among other erroneous opinions, was so deeply rooted that it would have been foolish, indeed impossible, to contest it openly in a popular lecture. But that Jesus is not supposed to have given to those who were destined to know the secrets of the Kingdom of God (Matt. 13: 11) any informative clue about this and that because of this the erroneous opinion was, as it were, sanctioned for centuries, even to the time of Thomasius, to the harm of humanity, that is incomprehensible to me. It would be high treason against humanity if--Jesus Himself had these better insights and the Evangelists narrate pure history. Was He Who came into the world to preach truth, Who preferred to die than act against His conviction supposed to have been intent on such an extremely foolish (<u>sit venia verbo</u>) sophistic wisdom? Certainly not. Do we prefer to see Jesus Himself as unknowing or have Him foolishly conceal what is right than admit that the entire demonology of the New Testament lay not in Jesus but in His later mythic biographers?

d) The silence of secular scribes becomes comprehensible. If in His lifetime Jesus had been such a well-known man, a prophet great in words and deeds as the Evangelists present Him, then it is quite striking that contemporary secular history does not even mention His setting. In Rome, the center of power and wisdom, one knew Jesus whom a Roman procurator had crucified, whom hundreds of Roman legionnaires must have heard and seen, so little that Suetonius, who lived under Trajan, has to have considered him a rebellious Jewish party walker under Claudius. (<u>Judeoas impulsore Chresto assidue tumultuantes etc</u>.) What is even more incomprehensible is that even the very vigilant Jewish historian does not known his almost contemporary landsman. The later age which felt these gaps, therefore, created the acts of

Pilate, a correspondence between Jesus and Abgarus, and a <u>testimonium</u> <u>Flavianum</u> which, however, criticism has thrown out in toto. For even the scholarly Bretschneider, who tried to save the testimony of Jesophus, was moved by Eichstaedt's sufficiently convincing reasons and gave up the bad egg; he will admit with us: "the secular scribes do not know Jesus;" to which I add: "because He never existed the way the evangelic history (the sacred saga) presents Him."

C. A third point of view from which the evangelic history tends to be considered is the mixed viewpoint. According to the ratio of components, it can be divided into the historical-mythical and the mythical-historical, depending on whether history or myth predominates. It has become popular in recent time and owes its origin to those theologians who cannot give up the history and yet are unable to find comfort with its clear results and think they can reconcile both parties with this middle course. A vain effort, which the strict supranaturalist will brand as heresy and the rationalist will ridicule! By trying to make comprehensible whatever is in any way possible, these mediators draw upon themselves all reproaches rightly made against natural history; and because they also allow for myth, the charge of inconsistency applies to them with all its gravity. And it weighs all the more since this accusation is the worst that can be made against a scholar, asserting as it does a contradiction within the author himself. Beyond that the procedure of these eclectics is the most arbitrary because they often decide according to very subjective reasons what should belong to myth and what to history. At least the Evangelists, logic, and the historical criticism appropriate to it know nothing of this. We now consider finally:

IV. the last consideration from and for which the history of Jesus can be treated. It is, namely, the great diversity of formal presentation which this very flexible material permits. There is almost no mode of presentation which would not be tried on this object and of which it would not be capable. Poets, orators, ascetics, historians, pedagogues all have mastered the material in their way and added of themselves. Thus, not only several ancients, e.g., Virgilius christianus, but also contemporaries like Klopstock and von Halem among others worked up the epic material to true epics. Ramler among others sang individual parts of the life of Jesus in cantatas; others dramatized it. The homilectic writers found here the most beautiful texts for edifying considerations. Hess and Greiling narrate rationally, but from different viewpoints and for different readers, the former verbosely, the latter in embellished lecture. Feddersen and Wilmsen, as well as the picture Bibles and biblical stories, are prepared for children, either for edification or as preparation for religious instruction, or also only for useful entertainment, each in his own way. Thus also the diversity of the form does not play less of a part in the constantly renewed revision of an object which inspires just such activity because of its material.

Heinz O. Guenther

# THE FOOTPRINTS OF JESUS' TWELVE IN EARLY CHRISTIAN TRADITIONS
A Study in the Meaning of Religious Symbolism

American University Studies: Series VII, Theology and Religion. Vol. 7.
ISBN 0-8204-0164-1        156 pp.        hardback US $ 20.90

The sudden disappearance of the twelve apostles from the pages of post-Easter Christian history is in B.H. Streeter's judgment 'one of the great mysteries of history'. The purpose of this publication is to shed some new light on this mystery and to examine, on the basis of the available New Testament evidence, the claim that the earthly Jesus himself had appointed the twelve. The book opens (Part I) with a redaction-critical inquiry into those New Testament writings which advance this claim, touching on both the origin and setting of the source materials used by the evangelists to support it. The question of how and why firmly established traditions are still suggestive enough to inspire visions entailing their reformulation on new levels of meaning is treated in this part. The book goes on (Part II) to discuss the role played by the symbolic number twelve in Hellenistic and Jewish milieux, concluding with the description of the substance and power added to early Christianity by the use of this prestigious number. The publication will be of benefit mostly to specialists and graduate students interested in deriving historical knowledge from religious materials.

PETER LANG PUBLISHING, INC.
62 West 45th Street
USA - New York, NY 10036

Heinz Bluhm

# LUTHER TRANSLATOR OF PAUL
Studies in Romans and Galatians

ISBN 0-8204-0186-2        595 pp.        hardback US $ 49.80

This book deals with selected passages from Luther's two favorite Pauline Epistles. Luther's renderings, from the *Septembertestament* of 1522 to the final revisions of 1546, are set in a framework extending from the pre-Lutheran Latin translations via the pre-Lutheran High and Low German Bibles as well as Emser's «Emendation» of the Luther New Testament to Luther's significant influence on the English Bible from Tyndale and Coverdale via the Authorized Version to the New English Bible.

Contents: The Zainer revision of the Mentel Bible — The Augsburg *Spiegel* of 1489 — The First English translation: Wicliffe — The Printed High German *Plenaria* and Luther's *Christmas Postil* — The Wittenberg 1529 revision of the Vulgate.

PETER LANG PUBLISHING, INC.
62 West 45th Street
USA – New York, NY 10036

| DATE DUE | | | |
|---|---|---|---|
| OCT 16 '98 | | | |
| | | | |
| | | | |
| | | | |
| | | | |
| | | | |
| | | | |
| | | | |
| | | | |
| | | | |
| | | | |
| | | | |
| | | | |
| | | | |
| | | | |

HIGHSMITH #LO-45220